SpringerBriefs in Social Work

SpringerBriefs present concise summaries of cutting-edge research and practical applications. Featuring compact volumes of 55 to 125 pages, the series covers a range of content from professional to academic. Typical topics might include:

- A timely report of state-of-the art analytical techniques
- A bridge between new research results, as published in journal articles, and a contextual literature review
- A snapshot of a hot or emerging topic
- An in-depth case study or clinical example
- A presentation of core concepts that students must understand in order to make independent contributions

SpringerBriefs in Social Work showcases emerging theory, empirical research, and practical applications in a wide variety of topics in social work and related areas. Briefs are characterized by fast, global electronic dissemination and expedited production schedules.

David Yuzva Clement • Ruxandra M. Gheorghe
Dennis Walkenhorst • Jade Hutchinson
Andrew McKenzie

Social Work and Countering Violent Extremism

Case Management, Direct Practice and Multi-Sectoral Collaboration

Springer

David Yuzva Clement
School of Social Work
Carleton University
Ottawa, ON, Canada

Ruxandra M. Gheorghe
School of Social Work
Carleton University
Ottawa, ON, Canada

Dennis Walkenhorst
Faculty of Social Work
IU International University of Applied Sciences
Leipzig, Germany

Jade Hutchinson
Department of Security Studies
Charles University
Prague, Praha, Czech Republic

Andrew McKenzie
Factor-Inwentash Faculty of Social Work
University of Toronto
Toronto, ON, Canada

ISSN 2195-3104 ISSN 2195-3112 (electronic)
SpringerBriefs in Social Work
ISBN 978-3-032-07085-2 ISBN 978-3-032-07086-9 (eBook)
https://doi.org/10.1007/978-3-032-07086-9

This Springer imprint is published by the registered company Springer Nature Switzerland AG
The registered company address is: Gewerbestrasse 11, 6330 Cham, Switzerland

Foreword

The public issues of extremism and risks of radicalisation are no longer private matters for a growing number of adults, children, and communities. Here in Aotearoa/New Zealand, like so many jurisdictions, we are grappling with the rise of younger children engaging in online spaces, where the attraction and excitement of extremism grows. Digital engagement has, indeed, become the new default, embedded in our daily lives. Their families and communities are a critical resource—a resource social work involves and welcomes to the table. They are our partners in practice. While other disciplines may take an atomised view of these issues, it is social work that holds family and community central and advocates for their inclusion. Working in countering violent extremism is hard work—it is emotional, demanding, and the subject matter perplexing.

This book offers a one-stop resource that explains the problems, defines the issues, and offers a range of practical ways we can assess and intervene to offset, as best we can, the scourge of radicalisation and extremism. This is an important and timely book, offering cogent arguments for the discipline of social work to lead, not to be determined by others, by drawing on our internationally ratified codes and ethics. This book is perhaps the first to offer such a comprehensive overview of social work practice and countering violent extremism.

I needed this book 10 years ago when my local authority grappled with the rise of securitization and police dominance in England, a time when just a few of us argued for social work to lead. Social work operates in each unique context. It is contemporary and yet must take its resolve from a shared set of ethics, rights, and equality arguments. Growing our practice evidence in social work regarding countering violent extremism will support a more confident position in how we effectively respond. This book will certainly help.

Oranga Tamariki
Wellington, Aotearoa/New Zealand

Tony Stanley

Acknowledgements

We sincerely appreciate the excellent, critical, and invaluable peer review feedback provided by our expert reviewers—Reza Ahmadi, Steve Barracosa, Mike King, Brett Kubicek, Kim McCalpin, Cécile Rousseau, Stephanie Scott-Smith, and Tony Stanley. Their thoughtful insights and careful critiques have greatly enhanced the depth, accuracy, and clarity of this book, strengthening its contributions to the field of social work. We also extend our deepest gratitude and appreciation to Springer Nature and, in particular, to Janet Kim, Dhivya Savariraj, and their team, for their exceptional support and thoughtful guidance throughout the entire writing and publishing process.

Competing Interests The authors have no competing interests to declare that are relevant to the content of this manuscript.

Contents

About the Authors

David Yuzva Clement, PhD, MSW, MA, RSW, is an Adjunct Research Professor at Carleton University's School of Social Work, an Associate Fellow at the International Centre for Counter-Terrorism, and a Research Advisor at the Canada Centre for Community Engagement and Prevention of Violence. His current research examines the nexus between social work and preventing and countering violent extremism; it also advances knowledge on children, youth, and families affected by violent extremism and extremist ideologies online, and explores the interplay between community organizing, civic education, and democracy. The views expressed in this book do not necessarily represent those of the Government of Canada.

Ruxandra M. Gheorghe, MSW, MA, RSW, is a Registered Social Worker and Research Advisor at the Canada Centre for Community Engagement and Prevention of Violence. She is also a Lecturer and Doctoral Candidate at Carleton University's School of Social Work. She is interested in intertwining the field of social work with preventing and countering violent extremism. Her current doctoral research is concerned with articulations of toxic masculinity in direct therapeutic practice. She has dedicated her research, practice, and advocacy to community well-being across multiple sectors in Canada and abroad. The views expressed in this book do not necessarily represent those of the Government of Canada.

Dennis Walkenhorst, PhD, MA, is a Professor of Social Work at the IU International University of Applied Sciences, Leipzig, Germany. His research examines countering violent extremism in social work, with a focus on case management, counselling, social diagnostics, and evaluation. From 2017 to 2023, he headed the Research Department at Violence Prevention Network and served as Founder and Scientific Director of the Center for Applied Research on Deradicalization (modus|zad) in Berlin.

Jade Hutchinson, PhD, MA, holds a Cotutelle Doctorate from the Department of Security Studies and Criminology at Macquarie University (Australia) and the Centre for Media and Journalism Studies at the University of Groningen (The Netherlands). Jade is currently a Post-Doctoral Fellow in the Department of Security Studies at Charles University (Czech Republic). Jade's research is focused on countering extremism and violence emerging from digital media ecosystems and understanding the effects of early childhood and adolescent exposure to online extremist materials. This work was supported by the Cooperatio program, research area Political Science.

Andrew McKenzie, MSW, RSW, has worked on the frontlines of the mental health and justice fields for over a decade. He first served as a Professional Assessor and Psychotherapist in youth and family mental health centres, conducting risk assessments for youth who had perpetrated sexual harm. For four years, he supervised Toronto's countering violent extremism program, Estimated Time of Arrival, an interdisciplinary team widely recognized for successfully rehabilitating individuals at risk of ideologically based violence. Andrew is now completing his PhD in Social Work at the University of Toronto, Canada, with a focus on training social workers to meet the rising challenge of a polarized population.

List of Authors

David Yuzva Clement, PhD, MSW, MA, RSW School of Social Work, Carleton University, Ottawa, ON, Canada

Ruxandra M. Gheorghe, MSW, MA, RSW School of Social Work, Carleton University, Ottawa, ON, Canada

Dennis Walkenhorst, PhD, MA IU International University of Applied Sciences, Leipzig, Germany

Jade Hutchinson, PhD, MA Department of Security Studies, Charles University, Prague, Czech Republic

Andrew McKenzie, MSW, RSW Factor-Inwentash Faculty of Social Work, University of Toronto, Toronto, ON, Canada

Chapter 1
Approaching Social Work and Countering Violent Extremism

1.1 Introduction

In an era marked by increasing social polarization, hate, and violent extremism, the role of social work within the realm of countering violent extremism (CVE) has never been more critical. This chapter reaffirms the overarching goal of this book: to illuminate the productive potential of social work when it is guided by critical, social justice-informed values and approaches. As psychosocial CVE interventions gain prominence across various sectors, there lies a vital opportunity to delve into the contributions of social work practice and scholarship in this space. This exploration is not only timely but essential, given the current landscape of rising extremism and the need for effective, compassionate responses.

At the time of writing, all authors of this book are actively engaged in working, researching, and teaching at the intersection of social work and CVE. Drawing on comparative reflections from Germany, Canada, and other contexts, our collective concerns about the securitization of the field have driven us to examine how social work can evolve in a manner that aligns with its core values and goals. This book emerges from a shared optimism about the potential for social work to contribute meaningfully to CVE, fostering a future where these efforts are grounded in social justice and community well-being, which are here understood as the pursuit of equity, inclusion, and human rights. Embedding CVE in a social justice framework ensures that interventions address complex and multivariate drivers of radicalization, including social polarization, marginalization, adverse childhood experiences, family trauma, and systemic inequality, to name but a few, rather than merely its symptoms. As societies grapple with the growing threat of radicalization and violent extremism, social workers are increasingly called upon to play a pivotal role in prevention and intervention efforts. This opening chapter underscores the critical importance of the social work profession within CVE initiatives. With social workers and other frontline practitioners in mental health and human services in mind,

D. Yuzva Clement et al., *Social Work and Countering Violent Extremism*, SpringerBriefs in Social Work, https://doi.org/10.1007/978-3-032-07086-9_1

this chapter provides a comprehensive introduction to the convergence of these two seemingly distant yet inherently interconnected fields. By examining the current state of the social work–CVE nexus, this chapter highlights existing scholarly research and explores the tensions and opportunities that frequently arise in this work. These include the conflicting securitization logics of risk and the necessity for a social work approach that is systems-focused, strengths-based, and trauma-informed, prioritizing client and community well-being. Equipped with practical concepts and theoretical frameworks, this chapter offers insights into how social work's guiding principles and systemic focus, spanning micro, meso, and macro levels, can be mobilized to better understand radicalization processes and counter violent extremism from a social work lens. This opening chapter concludes by outlining the objectives of this book, setting the stage for a deeper exploration of the dynamic and evolving role of social work in CVE.

This book largely focuses on the secondary and tertiary levels of prevention in countering violent extremism, emphasizing the critical role of social work in intervention and social reintegration. While primary prevention—directed at the general population, or subsets of the population, to ensure the development of problems is thwarted (*see* Chap. 3)—is acknowledged, the core of this book lies in understanding and enhancing responses once individuals are at-risk or already engaged in radicalization pathways.

1.2 Bridging the Gap: Social Work and Countering Violent Extremism (CVE)

As we write this book throughout 2024 and 2025, acts of hate and violent extremism continue to be orchestrated in our communities, online environments, and societies around the world. In its plainest form, *violent extremism* refers to the beliefs and behaviors of individuals and groups of people that support, espouse, and engage the use of harm to attain ideologically motivated goals, including religious, political, grievances related, and/or gendered goals. Relatedly, when an individual's or group's beliefs shift from being relatively conventional to being extreme, this shift is commonly known as *radicalization*. Radicalization does not necessarily mean that acts of physical violence will ensue. In fact, radicalization can generate both violent and non-violent behavior. To add, as historical events have shown, *radicalism* can result in positive societal change as well, such as the attainment of human rights. However, the moment when radicalized individuals or groups decide to mobilize acts of fear, violence, or terror for the purposes of attaining their ideological beliefs (e.g., political or social change), that behavior is then classified as violent extremism.

Violent extremism manifests in various ways, typically in the form of hate crimes,[1] support for violent groups or movements, terrorist violence, or even gender-based violence—such as with the so-called involuntary celibate (incel) movement, for instance. In addition to their most severe expressions, the impact of violent extremism generates widespread detrimental, traumatic, and intergenerational marks on societies, communities, families, and individuals, both young and old. We only need to look to our own metaphorical "backyards" to observe the multitude of violent extremist ideologies that dominate the current socio-political climate and fuel continued social polarization on both local and global levels. How to prevent and counter violent extremism is an undoubtedly timely and, indeed, necessary endeavor within the social work profession. What, then, is the role of the social work profession in general and social workers practicing in various social services and health care settings in particular when it comes to countering violent extremism?

The heart of this book emphasizes the critical role that social work can play within efforts to prevent and counter violent extremism. It is written to primarily support:

- Social workers and other frontline practitioners who work in a variety of practice fields, including generalist practice, child or youth services, child protection, family counseling, school social work, community work, private practice, correctional institutions or parole/probation services, mental health, and hospital social work
- Social workers and other frontline practitioners who specifically work as "CVE practitioners" in countering violent extremism intervention programs
- Researchers and lecturers interested in researching or teaching about the role of social work within preventing and countering radicalization and violent extremism, and
- Policymakers responsible for preventing and countering violent extremism program design and policy development

The overarching purpose of this book is to introduce the joining together of these two distant yet inherently interrelated fields: social work and countering violent extremism (CVE). After setting the stage for the role of the social work profession within the CVE sphere, this chapter maps existing research focusing on the CVE–social work nexus and offers several critical reflections on the challenges and opportunities of this work. Finally, this chapter ends by providing readers with an overview of the subsequent chapters covered in the remainder of this book.

[1] Although there is overlap between violent extremism and hate crimes, the two phenomena differ in significant respects (*see* Chap. 2).

1.3 Understanding the Intersection

In recent years, the fields of social work and countering violent extremism (CVE) have begun to converge—encouraging researchers, practitioners, and policymakers to recognize the intricate connections between individual and community well-being, socio-political dynamics, and violent extremism. For example, Staller (2019, p. 560) elaborated on this intersection and argued:

> In many ways, social workers are better equipped to disarm these movements than almost any other profession. We know something about the systems and institutions which fail [individuals], leaving them angry, isolated, and alienated. We know about trauma, historical trauma, and institutionalized racism. [...] These [individuals] are easily manipulated and their anger is exploitable by recruiters. However, there are also opportunities for social workers. If we are attentive to the spaces and places in which terrorism is born, we are in a position to dismantle, prevent and intervene before radicalization.

In its simplest terms, social work is dually understood as a relational practice-based profession as well as an academic discipline that works to advance individual, familial, community, and societal well-being (Hounmenou, 2012; Sheafor & Horejsi, 2006). Despite theoretical and practical similarities, social work is operationalized in different countries, regions, cultures, and organizations in diverse ways, including with regard to educational, legal, and methodological issues.[2] Indeed, there is a vast variety of theories, methods, and approaches applied within the scope of social work, and readers should be mindful that the guidance offered in this book might not be applicable in each and every context. Nevertheless, a large part of the social work profession operates within a long-established framework of social justice and advocacy that strives to address systemic inequalities and empower marginalized populations (Maylea et al., 2020). This values-based professional commitment to pursue social justice is grounded in a plethora of social work codes of ethics, guidelines, educational accreditation standards, and professional statements (e.g., CASW, 2005, 2020; CSWE, 2022; IFSW, 2014; NASW, 2016, 2021). According to the International Federation of Social Workers (IFSW, 2014), social work is globally understood to be: "a practice-based profession and an academic discipline that promotes social change and development, social cohesion, and the empowerment and liberation of people" (para. 2).

Social workers engage in various interventions to promote positive change, including counseling, advocacy, community organizing, and policy development. Although the social work profession is most often associated with clinical or direct practice on a micro level (e.g., between social work clinicians and clients or

[2] For example, in Canada social workers who hold graduate academic training (typically a *Master of Social Work*) are allowed to perform the act of psychotherapy, while in Germany this is not the case. Furthermore, in some Canadian provinces and territories graduate-level social workers with additional advanced clinical training are permitted to perform diagnoses based on the DSM-V, which is again not the case in Germany. And while social workers in Canada are mandated to be part of a licensing body and enroll in annual continued education, this level of professionalization is absent in Germany.

families), social workers are also frequently implicated in the meso and macro arenas of society. At the meso level, social workers practice within communities, groups, neighborhoods, and organizations—while oftentimes functioning as mediators between micro and macro domains of society (Finn, 2021). Social workers can also practice at the macro level and implicate themselves in broader structural advocacy and policy analysis at the organizational, governmental, and/or (inter)national level (Finn, 2021).

Although social work's scope is grounded in a vast range of theoretical frameworks and practice models (e.g., trauma-informed care, client-centered approaches, structural social work, anti-racist social work, Indigenous social work, and so forth; Finn, 2021; Hounmenou, 2012; Sheafor & Horejsi, 2006), what unites many of social work's approaches lies in its adoption of a systems-focused, social justice and ecological lens that holistically understands clients and communities as products within various micro, meso, and macro systems and contexts. Social work's theoretical framing is particularly helpful in examining the socio-political systems and historical contexts within environments that influence the well-being of people and communities. In other words, social work's structural focus not only works to better understand individuals and groups as simultaneously embedded in, impacting, and impacted by their socio-political contexts, but also has the productive potential to more comprehensively understand individuals and groups from a multitude of interrelated angles and forces. This process works to humanize individuals, help build their agency, and resist the pathological, risk- and deviance-focused assessments that are often prevalent in existing securitized and medicalized professions (Paré, 2014).

The fluidity of social work's systems-focused scope of practice, in combination with its guiding principles of social justice, renders social work a necessary profession to complement, and perhaps even guide, CVE spheres. Because social work navigates micro-level relational ruptures and macro-level structural exclusions, connects the two through an ecological logic that renders disengagement a matter of restoring rights, resources, and relational dignity, not merely recalibrating individual cognition and well-being. At the time of writing this book, several governments have already recognized that a whole-of-society approach is required to better understand, mitigate, and address the threat to safety that violent extremism and acts of hate generate. While several governments have traditionally placed emphasis on national security measures and law enforcement responses, much of these efforts have since evolved and broadened to place greater emphasis on multi-sectoral prevention practices and interventions—ones that are informed by public health paradigms aimed to provide an array of support services directed at individuals and groups involved in violent extremism (Hassan et al., 2021, 2022).

Countries like Germany have had a longer tradition of social work involvement in countering violent extremism, especially regarding right-wing extremism. For example, pioneering work with youth involved in right-wing extremist groups was developed under the leadership of Dr. Franz Josef Krafeld at the School of Social Work at Bremen University in (West) Germany in the late 1980s (Krafeld, 1992, 1996). Concepts like, what Krafeld called, "acceptance-based youth work," but also critical thinking, and person-in-environment, as well as theories stemming from group work and community organizing, were applied by Krafeld and his fellow social workers working with this population. Part of the so-called *Action-Program against Aggression and Violence*, implemented by the German federal government between 1992 and 1996, this predominantly youth-centered approach was then duplicated into Eastern Germany in the 1990s as a response to increased right-wing extremist organizing and several right-wing violent extremist attacks against immigrant communities and asylum centers. However, the way in which Krafeld's approach was implemented in East German contexts was problematic (Borrmann, 2019; Scherr, 2001). Krafeld repeatedly stressed that central components of his approach, such as building local awareness and resilience against rising right-wing extremism, to support youth developing critical thinking and alternative conflict resolution skills, and working alongside other community and civil society organizations to enculture youth in alternative environments, were simply ignored. As a result, in some instances in Eastern Germany, social work had in fact contributed to right-wing extremist organizing, instead of preventing or countering it (Borrmann, 2019). This led to a heated debate within German social work regarding how to best prevent and counter right-wing extremism. For example, Krafeld was critiqued by his contemporaries for aiming to solve larger political issues through social work, or simply for ignoring political (i.e., far-right) ideology altogether by emphasizing the complex social issues that underpinned radicalization pathways. Research had found that Krafeld's acceptance-based approach, developed by drawing on similar relational and non-judgmental methods in social work with people who use substances, was effective in contexts where right-wing extremist groups were isolated and civil society organizations actively involved in local anti-racist work against right-wing extremism (Drilling & Davolio, 2004; Scherr, 2001). As a result, emphasis on *context*, the *social environment*, and *milieu* became the focal point for CVE interventions directed against right-wing extremism, with work unfolding with parents, in youth centers, neighborhoods, and communities aimed at better understanding levels of tolerance toward racist and extremist attitudes, depriving right-wing extremism of its breeding ground, and intervening within the social environment of vulnerable youth. Individually tailored, case management approaches were, back then, not yet adopted when working with this population.

At the same time, in the early 2000s, the German federal government began to fund prison-based CVE programs. During this period, right-wing extremist networks became a significant problem in many prisons, particularly in states such as Brandenburg in Eastern Germany. In response to this challenge, non-governmental organizations (NGOs), such as Violence Prevention Network, initiated various intervention programs within correctional contexts working with violent extremist inmates, many of whom had been sentenced for violent crimes including murder. The programs offered anti-aggression and anti-violence training, individual counseling, and group sessions. These initiatives adapted Krafeld's acceptance-based approach for the specific context of prisons and the target demographic of ideologically (e.g., far-right) motivated violent offenders. Around 2007, these programs were subsequently adapted to address religiously motivated violent offenders in prisons.

Similar to their German counterparts, countries like Switzerland had seen analogous trends in right-wing extremism and social work was called upon to work with at-risk youth, parents, teachers, labor unions, neighborhoods, and communities, as well as in correctional settings (Drilling & Davolio, 2004). In North America, CVE efforts were most often born out of national security and counter-terrorism spaces and policies in the post-9/11 era (Hutson, 2021; Kubicek & King, 2021). In this light, CVE was, and sometimes still is, understood as a "soft" sub-field of counter-terrorism. However, since 2016, Canada has seen increased investment into psychosocial intervention programs that work with individuals at-risk of or who have become involved in violent extremism. These programs, understood as distinct but complementary of law enforcement and national security efforts, are in most cases anchored in community-based social service agencies and NGOs where social workers and other psychosocial professionals are at the forefront of working with individuals and families (including in correctional contexts) in order to build protective factors and divert them from pathways toward violent extremism (Kubicek & King, 2021). As well, the Canadian Practitioners Network for the Prevention of Extremist Violence (CPN-PREV) was established in 2017 in Canada with the aim to conduct research and to provide knowledge mobilization and capacity building; in 2020, CPN-PREV established a *community of practice* for those practitioners working in CVE intervention programs across Canada (CPN-PREV, n.d.).

Similarly, the United States has seen an increased focus on preventing domestic terrorism and targeted violence in recent years (Koehler, 2022). The U.S. Department of Homeland Security's (DHS) Centre for Prevention Programs and Partnerships (CP3), created in 2021, set out a new prevention framework and funding apparatus to address various forms of violent extremism grounded in a whole-of-society approach. It builds on DHS' earlier work to support CVE research, as well as integrating lessons learned from prison-based CVE programs that were piloted in some U.S. states (Koehler, 2022). For instance, this includes a pilot project that was launched in 2016 and spearheaded at the U.S. District Court for the District of Minnesota in Minneapolis which integrated probation services and training for probation officers with community-based rehabilitation services aimed at disengagement from violent extremism (Koehler, 2022). Similar to CPN-PREV, the Prevention Practitioners Network (PPN) provides services, events, capacity building, and practice guides to professionals from different sectors in the United States working in targeted violence and terrorism prevention (PPN, n.d.).

Upon closer examination, it becomes evident that CVE and social work share common goals and principles. Both fields are concerned with addressing underlying social issues, promoting inclusivity and resilience, and fostering positive social change in a context of polarization and conflict as well as the experience of injustice and grievance. We have hence moved away from merely asking whether an intersection between social work and CVE exists, and instead moved toward asking what that intersection looks like, in what ways it currently operates, and what critical challenges and opportunities lie within it. Within existing policies and programming, social workers will be or already are key actors involved in CVE efforts which are often coined by multi-sectoral collaboration. Particularly from an assessment and intervention perspective, social work offers a theoretically comprehensive foundation to operate in the multimodal CVE environment (Finch et al., 2019; Regehr & Glancy, 2014).

The nexus between social work and CVE lies in the focus on individual and community well-being during times of societal distress and socio-political polarization. We know that social work takes a holistic and humanistic approach, addressing the interconnectedness of individual, family, community, and societal factors. Similarly, the CVE sphere must consider the complex web of influences shaping radicalization and societal instability, including political, economic, psychosocial, historical, and digital dimensions. Staller (2019) encouraged social workers to reconstruct "seemingly random individualized tragedies—what [Staller] calls 'private woes'—into publicly recognized problems which highlight the commonality of experiences" (pp. 558–559). By reframing violent harms as symptoms of broader social problems, social work then becomes a prime profession to delve into this work. Social workers recognize that vulnerabilities such as low socioeconomic status (SES), discrimination, trauma, and alienation can increase susceptibility to extremist ideologies and deviant behavior. By addressing these underlying factors, social work interventions can help mitigate the risk of radicalization and promote alternative pathways for individuals and groups at risk of violent extremism or whom are already involved in such harmful acts.

1.4 Mapping the Social Work and CVE Nexus: Existing Research

While radicalization, violent extremism and associated societal harms are pressing issues, and although multi-sectoral collaboration and international knowledge exchange regarding CVE have significantly increased in recent decades, the documented role of social work in this realm is emerging and largely unclear. From an international viewpoint, in the *Palgrave Handbook of Global Social Work Education*, Sajid and colleagues reported that irrespective of economic development, societies around the world are facing "incidents of violence, terrorism, and attacks on human dignity and life" (2020, p. 7). Social workers, the authors continued, must hence be trained to advocate for social justice, counter these threats, and harness the knowledge and skills to "deal with extremist powers and socially deviant behaviour" (Sajid et al., 2020, p. 7). At the same time, guiding social work principles, such as trauma-informed and strengths-based frameworks, are being applied within countering violent extremism scholarship (Marsden & Lewis, 2021; Marsden & Lee, 2022).

In practice, although social workers are more and more called upon by governments to assist and intervene with cases of radicalization and violent extremism, much of the empirical and conceptual work on the social work–CVE nexus is marginal in existing scholarship. However, some authors have begun to situate social work within broader CVE work and, through their writings, have suggested that CVE is an emerging sub-field in social work (Birdwell, 2020; Frounfelker et al., 2023; Heesh, 2022; Hutson, 2021; Jakob et al., 2023). Exploring how social workers in the United Kingdom working in schools and local authorities have been engaged in risk assessment for radicalization cases, Stanley and Guru (2015) proposed four central areas of upskilling needed for social workers in social services roles engaged in radicalization assessment and interventions:

1. Family work skills (family dynamics, power structures, involvement of extended family members, ecomapping, and genogram tools)
2. Political, violent extremism, and ideological analysis skills (understanding extremist ideologies and scenes, understanding their appeal, needs-oriented analyses of radicalization processes)
3. Sophisticated risk and needs assessment skills that understand risk to radicalization and violent extremism in nuanced, contextualized, and systemic ways—rather than the narrow, punitive, and pathologizing risk lens historically upheld in CVE, and
4. Developing *sociological imagination*, person-in-context, and understanding historical and structural factors related to today's contexts

By referring to Birdwell (2020) who underscored the role of online social work interventions to counter violent extremism, we can add a *fifth* skill dimension: to effectively reach vulnerable audiences online and the role of digital social work, a field that has received increased attention and seen program development throughout the past few years (e.g., Moonshot, 2023; *see* Chap. 2).

Later on in 2021, Hutson was among the first scholars to intertwine the focus on countering violent extremism with the field of social work in the United States. Hutson (2021) expressed that social work would greatly complement CVE efforts given its rich practice history focusing on violence prevention in other similar contexts, including sexual assault and abuse, gang violence, and other violence-intense contexts. Several other authors have similarly called for social work's stronger involvement in CVE, both in research and in practice, due to social work's ability to understand radicalization and its multi-faceted root causes in more nuanced and structurally sound ways (Heesh, 2022; Staller, 2019). While few qualitative studies have been specifically published on this nexus, Haugstvedt's (2019) interviews and focus groups with Norwegian social workers in the CVE field found that their ability to reframe pathways to radicalization as "a social problem" (p. 158) allowed frontline practitioners to overcome uncertainty and rely on their social work training, knowledge, and intervention approaches. This is similar to Krafeld (1992, 1996) who advocated for this perspective earlier in Germany; in Krafeld's later writings we see references to Amartya Sen and Martha Nussbaum's capabilities approach aimed at improving individual and structural opportunities and conditions that enable active realization of potential, and viewing individuals as powerful agents for change (Krafeld, 2016). Stanley et al. (2018) furthermore stressed the need for family-based

CVE interventions (*see* Chap. 4). These authors referred to the Good Lives Model (i.e., a humanistic approach to offender rehabilitation) and family group conferencing as examples of how to apply strengths- and needs-based as well as multi-systemic approaches toward radicalization. In the Canadian context, McKenzie and O'Brien (2024) also discussed the role of graduate-level social workers in a Toronto-based CVE intervention program who use their competencies in psychotherapeutic modalities such as Cognitive Behavioral Therapy, Dialectical Behavior Therapy, and Motivational Interviewing to support clients in direct practice.

Other scholars exploring protective factors against radicalization to violent extremism have stressed that social work as a discipline has both the capacity and scope to foster resilience against and rehabilitation from violence through its interventions, especially when implemented alongside other multi-modal and interdisciplinary intervention efforts (Hassan et al., 2021; Lösel et al., 2018). Rather than focusing on mitigating just one cause and driver, multi-modal CVE efforts that target the broader social ecology, needs, and life-course adversities of clients are deemed to be more effective because they can address multi-factorial radicalization pathways in tandem (Eisenman et al., 2020; Lösel et al., 2018; McKenzie & O'Brien, 2024). When put into practice, previous studies have shown that disengagement from violent extremism and rehabilitation or social reintegration is seldom a linear process, but rather it is an interplay between assessing risk factors, adversities, and protective factors in context, working to address unmet needs, encouraging resilience, and building individualized, family, or community protective factors that work to promote both cognitive-behavioral change and social cohesion (Hassan et al., 2021, 2022; Horgan et al., 2020).

These findings are corroborated by another study that underscored the need for holistic multi-systemic intervention approaches (Kolbe, 2019). Kolbe, who evaluated a secondary CVE program in an East African city that targeted youth at-risk of radicalization and recruitment into Al-Shabaab, found that a comprehensive intervention approach consisting of a) group sessions, b) recreational activities and civic education, and c) individually tailored home-based social work services was more effective to prevent attachment and recruitment into Al-Shabaab among program participants compared to youth that only received group sessions (Kolbe, 2019). In this program, home-based interventions followed a multi-systemic framework and included family therapy, case management and advocacy, social support for clients and their families in terms of school attachment and vocational training, and transportation services.

Interestingly, Birdwell (2020) underscored the need to develop a new field of *intervention science* for CVE that triangulates and codifies the experience and expertise of social workers, mental health specialists, and former extremists themselves. The author argued that this development, however, must be rooted in the critical social work ethics and values illustrated above, otherwise risking an overreliance on risk-based approaches that are often replicated in counter-terrorism and law enforcement spheres. In a similar vein, Walkenhorst argued to utilize theories and approaches that emerged within social work history and discourse, instead of decoupling CVE research, theory, and practice development from social work scholarship (Walkenhorst, 2022). Key examples of such theories include strengths-based approaches, trauma-informed approaches, empowerment, family-oriented social work, social ecology, community development, social diagnostics, and case management, which are part of the social work tradition and foundational within social work's vast scope of theory and practice (Gitterman & Germain, 1976; Kurtz et al., 1984; Leukefeld, 1990; Leverson, 2017; Saleebey, 1996; Sheafor & Horejsi, 2006; Solomon, 1987). This understanding, then, presents a unique opportunity to bridge the two fields and consider CVE as an emerging new field of social work.

1.5 Competing Agents? Critical Reflections, Challenges, and Opportunities

At this point, readers may be wondering how social work can navigate its commitment to social justice and anti-oppression while working within an inherently securitized field of practice—one that seems to be antithetical, if not, contradictory to core social work values, goals, and principles. It must undoubtedly be taken into account that while the integration of social work into CVE holds fruitful promise, it also poses unique challenges and ethical dilemmas due to its complex nature and intersection with various societal issues. One of the most prominent examples lies within the very concept of radicalization as well as its counterpart, deradicalization. Some scholars have critiqued that these concepts were coined as a result of national security and counter-terrorism discourses with the intention of strengthening state control, policing, and law enforcement (Amadeu Antonio Stiftung, 2016). Far from the community mental health approaches and social justice-focused theories of social work, such concepts unfold under the assumption of *pre-criminal* or *non-criminal* states of being and, as such, have been thought to infringe on the guaranteed rights and freedoms of persons, groups, and communities. This has particularly been the case with Muslim communities which have seen heightened criminalization, securitization, and surveillance under the guise of public safety (Ahmad, 2020; Awan, 2012; Yassine & Briskman, 2019). The construction of so-called *suspect communities* has run the risk of stigmatizing entire groups and communities, unfairly targeting individuals based on their positionalities or identities, and further marginalizing communities as security threats—outcomes that prove to be far from the goals that social work proclaims and hopes to operate within.

Securitization continues to be a major point of contention due to its risk discourses that can generate negative unintended effects on the very clients and communities it aims to support. For instance, in discussing social work within CVE efforts in the United Kingdom and Sweden, Finch et al. (2019) cautioned how close proximity to securitization and its associated risk paradigm can undermine the very social justice and community empowerment values and ethical pillars that social work seeks. Exploring this securitization and social work dichotomy, McKendrick and Finch (2017) posited that the active and reflexive engagement with risk discourses can be incredibly beneficial for CVE spaces; however, the authors stressed that it is of upmost importance for these interventions to be anchored in social work theories and methods, and not a reproduction or adoption of existing securitized logics. Other authors have similarly concluded that although social workers certainly have a critical role to play in the arena of CVE practice, it is of upmost importance for social workers to resist the tendency toward risk-aversion and risk-work by refocusing on strengths-based perspectives (Stanley et al., 2017). Due to the fact that ensuring public safety is a field that often involves law enforcement and security agencies, social workers are encouraged to be critical of securitization logics and mindful of their role and mandate in multi-agency practice settings (*see* Chap. 4).

It is in this context that existing social work scholarship regarding CVE repeatedly points toward *blurred roles* that can occur when securitization and social care logics are blended. Namely, the goals of risk-focused CVE efforts and the goals of social care greatly differ, and hence social workers navigating these tensions undoubtedly identified a plethora of ethical dilemmas including the participation in and reproduction of colonial ideas (Finch et al., 2019), individualization practices of adopting unnuanced and unidimensional perspectives of clients (Borrmann, 2019), and *bracketing off* these tensions by minimizing or dismissing risks surrounding radicalization and delegating CVE away from social work (Chivers, 2018). More so, other authors have also documented social workers within CVE spaces who espoused misinformation and misunderstandings regarding client behaviors (McKendrick & Finch, 2017), reproduced securitization, discriminatory and oppressive practices toward racialized clients and families (Haugstvedt, 2022; Radvan, 2010; Stanley & Guru, 2015), and even social workers who have adopted racist or far-right views themselves while working with these clients (Borrmann, 2019).

Several social work scholars cited in this chapter have suggested two avenues to resist securitization and bias. First, to apply and communicate core social work principles (such as trust-building, rapport, confidentiality, and non-judgmental communication with clients, alongside social justice, anti-racism, and anti-oppression frameworks), and second, to ensure and mobilize social support, supervision, and peer-to-peer mentorship among social work practitioners engaged in CVE to advance their own critical reflection and well-being when working with clients and engaging in multi-agency collaboration.

Notably, this work can be taxing and challenging, especially when engaging with clients who communicate extremist beliefs and hatred (Krafeld, 1992; Radvan, 2010). Some social workers, who may lack a concrete understanding of their own countertransference, social positionality, and personal values, may find it difficult supporting clients who subscribe to extremist ideologies. This is particularly apparent when the clients' extremist belief systems and behaviors are inherently against practitioners' own beliefs, values, and even identities as well as contrary to social work ethics overall (IFSW, 2014). Relatedly, an added challenge arises when a social worker, or a part of the social worker's identity (e.g., race, sexual orientation, ability, and so on), is targeted by the client and the ideology the client subscribes to. Consider, for instance, a racialized social worker supporting a white supremacist client. This social worker might find it challenging to build rapport and work through the client's projections while being the subject of the client's hatred or discrimination (Bartoli & Pyati, 2009). This discomfort is amplified if social workers do not possess a strong self-awareness or reflexivity of their personal and professional values, tolerance levels and triggers in relation to clients, if they are unprepared to self-regulate, and/or lack professional support systems (e.g., supervision, team processing) when exposed to such issues that arise when supporting radicalized clients.

General research on challenges and opportunities regarding the client–practitioner relationship offers insightful guidance. For practicing social workers, there is harm that can arise from these tensions. Wolf et al. (2017) found that clinicians who cannot adequately regulate their negative reactions to clients may cause harm to clients and their therapeutic alliance through their dysregulation. Other scholars agreed, claiming that unmanaged clinician frustration, anxiety, and dysregulation thwart clinicians from being fully able to recognize and cope with their reactions and, by extension, prevent clinicians from authentically engaging and understanding the client (Bartoli & Pyati, 2009; Green, 2006; Groshong, 2013). Bartoli and Pyati (2009) explored the issue of supporting clients in direct practice who espouse racist and prejudicial comments. The authors encouraged practitioners to be mindful of their own anxiety or motivations, investigate the meaning behind the client's statements, support the client's reflexivity in how those projections reflect the client's views of themself, and then draw on these insights to help the client attain their goals (Bartoli & Pyati, 2009). Within the context of supporting anti-Semitic clients, Radvan (2010) suggested to neither debate, counter-argue, nor engage in ideological discussions, but to reconstruct the client's sense-making, context, and trajectory into radicalization. Furthermore, Motivational Interviewing (MI) emphasizes a collaborative therapeutic relationship between practitioner and client with the aim to enhance client motivation toward readiness, growth, and behavior change; here, the practitioner is viewed as a facilitator and not as an expert (Clark, 2019). In this context, the basic principles of Carl Rogers' person-centered therapy approach, such as empathy, unconditional positive regard, and congruence, are central to working with radicalized individuals. Empathy enables practitioners to understand the personal experiences and emotions of these individuals and foster a sense of being heard and valued. Unconditional positive regard involves accepting individuals without judgment and creating a safe space for open dialogue, although this does not imply validating extremist attitudes, viewpoints, and violence. Congruence, or authenticity, ensures that practitioners remain genuine and build trusting relationships with clients. Evaluation of CVE programs suggests that person-centered therapy is a useful approach for intervention programming (McKenzie & O'Brien, 2024; Uhlmann, 2017). For example, the German Federal Office for Migration and Refugees (BAMF) emphasized the importance of empathetic and non-judgmental communication for its counseling services for radicalized individuals. Their program evaluation found that applying this approach increased the effectiveness of interventions aimed at disengagement from violent extremism (Uhlmann, 2017).

Trauma-informed and culturally sensitive practice help prevent further harm in both CVE and non-CVE contexts. Key components of trauma-informed care include for staff and organizations to implement principles such as trustworthiness, choice, and empowerment (Leverson, 2017). In this person-responsive context, clients can bring their whole selves to treatment and have greater opportunity for success. To do so, scholars have encouraged clinicians, including in CVE, to engage in self-reflective work, personal therapy, and supervision and peer support in an effort to better understand themselves (including personal and professional values and roles), their body's cues, and their reactions to clients they may have a strong reaction to (Gelso & Hayes, 2002, 2007; Haugstvedt, 2022; Wolf et al., 2013). Further, an emerging best practice for multidisciplinary teams is engaging in a co-therapy or co-practice model (McKenzie & O'Brien, 2024; Roller & Nelson, 1991), wherein one client or family is supported by multiple social workers, outreach workers, and/or caseworkers simultaneously. These team-based approaches have been a promising approach to CVE direct practice and could serve as an effective support system for social workers in the CVE realm while simultaneously reducing the risk of workplace isolation and burnout (McKenzie & O'Brien, 2024).

When taken together, we remind social workers within the CVE sphere to hold close the social work values and methods that embolden reflexive practice, critical consciousness, intersectional anti-oppressive frameworks, and social justice. It is these very tenets of social work that render the profession to play a critical role within CVE, particularly in its ability to question taken-for-granted dogmas, challenge dominant discourses that reproduce harm, and reframe and re-evaluate experiences from more nuanced perspectives. Moreover, social work's experience in areas like gang prevention, intimate partner violence, and sexual offending offers valuable insights for CVE. Drawing on ecological systems theory (Heise, 1998), social work emphasizes holistic, multi-level assessment and integrated interventions for the context of gender-based violence. Practices such as wraparound supports, restorative justice, and individualized case management—used in gang prevention in South Africa (Jongh, 2021), with sex offenders in Canada and the United Kingdom (Thomas et al., 2014), and alongside group work with men who perpetrate intimate partner violence (Augusta Scott, 2009, 2016)—can inform CVE strategies. These approaches mobilize protective factors, address root causes, and foster resilience through multi-sectoral collaboration.

1.6 Conclusion: Objective of this Book and Guiding Principles

This chapter has come full circle to reaffirm the goal of this very book: to highlight the productive potential of social work within CVE when undertaken using critical, social justice-informed values and approaches. As social polarization, hate, and violent extremism continue to rise and countering violent extremism interventions continue to receive increased attention across sectors, herein lies a vital opportunity to explore the role of social work practice and scholarship in this space. What the social work and CVE nexus currently looks like, the role it can play, and the imaginative future we want it to look like as the CVE sphere continues to develop certainly warrants further exploration. At the time of writing this book, all authors are working, researching, and teaching within this intersection. This book dually transpired from our collective concerns about the securitization of the field, but also from our shared optimism about how this field can further develop in a critical way that aligns with the social work values and goals that continue to serve as our compass. Echoing the existing research that we explored throughout this chapter, we believe the following guiding principles—which will be further explored throughout this book—are key to advancing countering violent extremism from a social work perspective:

- The role of collaborative **multi-systemic** and **social-ecological approaches** in comprehensive and psychosocial client-centered CVE interventions, and the need to learn from other professions and fields of practice
- The need to apply **person-in-environment, strengths-based,** and **trauma-informed practice** to adequately address complex histories and contextualize them in socio-political contexts, attend to a variety of traumatic experiences, and engage unmet needs and challenges that contribute to radicalization pathways, violence, or risk
- Drawing from the pool of **family-based intervention approaches**, considering family members and caregivers, alongside other professionals (e.g., teachers, youth workers, correctional staff) as clients and intervention partners within broader client-systems
- Prioritizing **professional social support and well-being for practitioners** through supervision, peer mentorship, communities of practice, continued learning, self-compassion, and so forth
- Working to **develop distinct clarification** between securitization and social justice/social care logics in CVE, creating clear boundaries within multi-sectoral contexts and fostering mutual understanding, and relatedly
- **Centering foundational social work codes of ethics** to guide critical practitioner reflexivity, the promotion of social justice and anti-oppressive practice (AOP), confidentiality, and striving toward critical consciousness and anti-bias approaches toward CVE to avoid reproducing stigmatizing language and behaviors which have plagued the CVE field

With this in mind, Chap. 2 outlines focal elements of radicalization and violent extremism, including key (and contested) definitions and existing models. Chapter 3 introduces processes of exit and disengagement from radicalization, especially in relation to case management and the direct practice role of social workers supporting clients who distance themselves from violent extremism. Chapter 4 examines tensions and challenges in multi-sectoral/interagency collaboration, provides an overview of youth violent radicalization and family issues, and also discusses CVE in correctional and criminal justice contexts. Finally, a summary chapter (Chap. 5) concludes our book by providing a summation of the aforementioned chapters, outlining key implications, and suggesting steps forward. We hope that the following chapters will help pave the emerging road for social work within CVE.

References

Ahmad, F. (2020). The securitization of Muslim civil society in Canada. In D. M. D. Silva & M. Deflem (Eds.), *Radicalization and counter-radicalization, sociology of crime, law and deviance* (pp. 115–133). Emerald Publishing Limited.

Amadeu Antonio Stiftung. (2016). *A critique of "deradicalization."* The task force on gendered right-wing extremism prevention. Retrieved March 11, 2025, from https://www.amadeu-antonio-stiftung.de/wp-content/uploads/2019/01/deradicalization.pdf.

Augusta Scott, T. (2016). Stopping violence against women: Wade's story. In S. Hick & J. Stokes (Eds.), *Social work in Canada: An introduction* (4th ed., pp. 264–265). Thompson Publishing.

Augusta Scott, T. (2009). A narrative therapy approach to conversations with men about perpetrating abuse. In P. Lehmann & C. Simmons (Eds.), *Strengths based batterers intervention: A new paradigm in ending family violence* (pp. 113–135). Springer Press.

Awan, I. (2012). 'I am a Muslim not an extremist': How the prevent strategy has constructed a 'suspect' community. *Politics & Policy, 40*(6), 1158–1185. https://doi.org/10.1111/j.1747-1346.2012.00397.x

Bartoli, E., & Pyati, A. (2009). Addressing clients' racism and racial prejudice in individual psychotherapy: Therapeutic considerations. *Psychotherapy: Theory, Research, Practice, Training, 46*(2), 145–157. https://doi.org/10.1037/a0016023

Birdwell, J. (2020). Developing effective and ethical 'secondary' intervention programmes to counter radicalisation and polarisation. In M. Littler & B. Lee (Eds.), *Digital extremisms: Palgrave studies in cybercrime and cybersecurity* (pp. 197–222). Palgrave Macmillan. https://doi.org/10.1007/978-3-030-30138-5_10

Borrmann, S. (2019). Ethical dilemmas when working with extreme right-winged youth cultures in Germany. In S. Marson & R. McKenney (Eds.), *The Routledge handbook of social work ethics and values* (pp. 206–214). Routledge.

CASW. (2005). *Code of ethics.* Canadian Association of Social Workers. Retrieved March 11, 2025, from http://casw-acts.ca/sites/default/files/attachements/casw_code_of_ethics.pdf.

CASW. (2020). *Scope of practice statement.* Canadian Association of Social Workers. Retrieved March 11, 2025, from https://www.casw-acts.ca/files/attachements/Scope_of_Practice_Statement_2020_1.pdf.

Chivers, C. (2018). "What is the headspace they are in when they are making those referrals?" Exploring the lifeworlds and experiences of health and social care practitioners undertaking risk work within the prevent strategy. *Health, Risk & Society, 20*(1–2), 81–103. https://doi.org/10.1080/13698575.2018.1437121

Clark, M. D. (2019). Motivational interviewing for deradicalization: Increasing the readiness to change. *Journal for Deradicalization, 20*, 47–74. https://journals.sfu.ca/jd/index.php/jd/article/view/245/169

CPN-PREV. (n.d.). *About us.* Canadian Practitioners Network for the Prevention of Extremist Violence (CPN-PREV). Retrieved March 11, 2025, from https://cpnprev.ca/about-us.

CSWE. (2022). *Educational policy and accreditation standards for baccalaureate and master's social work programs (EPAS).* Council on Social Work Education. Retrieved July 9, 2025, from https://www.cswe.org/getmedia/bb5d8afe-7680-42dc-a332-a6e6103f4998/2022-EPAS.pdf.

Drilling, M., & Davolio, M. E. (Eds.) (2004). *Rechtsextremismus und Soziale Arbeit.* Verlag Fachhochschule für Soziale Arbeit Beider Basel. Retrieved March 11, 2025, from https://edudoc.ch/record/28809/files/rechtsextremismus.pdf.

Eisenman, D., Weine, S., & Lashley, M. (2020). Can public health help prevent violent extremism? Should public health help prevent violent extremism? In S. V. Hlatky (Ed.), *Countering violent extremism and terrorism: Assessing domestic and international strategies* (pp. 47–63). McGill-Queen's University Press.

Finch, J., Jönsson, J. H., Kamali, M., & McKendrick, D. (2019). Social work and countering violent extremism in Sweden and the UK. *European Journal of Social Work, 25*(1), 119–130. https://doi.org/10.1080/13691457.2019.1657803

Finn, J. L. (2021). *Just practice: A social justice approach to social work*. Oxford University Press.
Frounfelker, R. L., Johnson-Lafleur, J., Montmagny Grenier, C., Duriesmith, D., & Rousseau, C. (2023). "Between the self and the other": Clinical presentation of male supremacy in violent extremists. *Behavioral Sciences of Terrorism and Political Aggression*, 1–21. https://doi.org/10.1080/19434472.2023.2185277
Gelso, C. J., & Hayes, J. A. (2002). Countertransference management. *Psychotherapy: Theory, Research, Practice, Training, 38*(4), 418–422. https://doi.org/10.1037/0033-3204.38.4.418
Gelso, C. J., & Hayes, J. A. (2007). *Countertransference and the therapist's inner experience: Perils and possibilities*. Lawrence Erlbaum Associates, Publishers.
Gitterman, A., & Germain, C. B. (1976). Social work practice: A life model. *Social Service Review, 50*(4), 601–610. https://doi.org/10.1086/643430
Green, L. B. (2006). The value of hate in the countertransference. *Clinical Social Work Journal, 34*(2), 187–199. https://doi.org/10.1007/s10615-005-0008-2
Groshong, L. W. (2013). Politics in the consulting room: Hate in the countertransference revisited. *Clinical Social Work Journal, 41*(1), 43–49. https://doi.org/10.1007/s10615-011-0371-0
Hassan, G., Brouillette-Alarie, S., Ousman, S., Savard, É. L., Kilinc, D., Madriaza, P., Varela, W., Pickup, D., Danis, E., & The CPN-PREV Team. (2021). *A systematic review on the outcomes of tertiary prevention programs in the field of violent radicalization*. Canadian Practitioners Network for the Prevention of Radicalization and Extremist Violence. Retrieved March 11, 2025, from https://cpnprev.ca/systematic-review-3/.
Hassan, G., Madriaza, P., Brouillette-Alarie, S., Danis, E., Varela, W., Ousman, S., Kilinc, D., Savard, É. L., Lavoie, L., & The CPN-PREV Team. (2022). *Guidelines for the prevention of violent extremism online and offline: Findings from the expert conference and the Delphi consensus process*. Canadian Practitioners Network for the Prevention of Radicalization and Extremist Violence. Retrieved March 11, 2025, from https://cpnprev.ca/guideline-committees.
Haugstvedt, H. (2019). Trusting the mistrusted: Norwegian social workers' strategies in preventing radicalization and violent extremism. *Journal for Deradicalization, 19*, 149–184. https://journals.sfu.ca/jd/index.php/jd/article/view/219
Haugstvedt, H. (2022). The role of social support for social workers engaged in preventing radicalization and violent extremism. *Nordic Social Work Research, 12*(1), 166–179. https://doi.org/10.1080/2156857X.2020.1806102
Heesh, A. (2022). Why it should be us: The case for social work to lead alt-right radicalisation interventions. *Social Work & Policy Studies: Social Justice, Practice and Theory, 5*(2), 1–15. https://openjournals.library.sydney.edu.au/SWPS/article/view/17115.
Heise, L. (1998). Violence against women: An integrated ecological framework. *Violence Against Women, 4*(3), 262–290. https://doi.org/10.1177/1077801298004003002
Horgan, J., Meredith, K., & Papatheodorou, K. (2020). Does deradicalization work? In D. M. D. Silva & M. Deflem (Eds.), *Radicalization and counter-radicalization* (Vol. 25, pp. 9–20). Emerald Publishing Limited. https://doi.org/10.1108/S1521-613620200000025001
Hounmenou, C. (2012). Black settlement houses and oppositional consciousness. *Journal of Black Studies, 43*(6), 646–666. https://doi.org/10.1177/0021934712441203
Hutson, R. A. (2021). Preventing violent extremism and social work: Recent US history and prospects. *Journal of Human Rights and Social Work, 6*, 298–306. https://doi.org/10.1007/s41134-021-00177-x
International Federation of Social Workers. (2014). *Global definition of social work*. Retrieved March 11, 2025, from https://www.ifsw.org/what-is-social-work/global-definition-of-social-work/.
Jakob, M., Jukschat, N., & Leistner, A. (2023). The paradoxes of social work in a securitised setting: the example of prevention and radicalisation in German prisons. *International Journal of Social Pedagogy, 12*(1). https://doi.org/10.14324/111.444.ijsp.2023.v12.x.003
Jongh, S. L. D. (2021). *The views of social workers regarding their role in youth gang prevention in communities of the western cape*. Stellenbosch University. Retrieved March 11, 2025, from http://hdl.handle.net/10019.1/123627

Koehler, D. (2022). A tale of two worlds: The United States of America's efforts to prevent terrorism recruitment and extremist violence. In R. Ceylan & M. Kiefer (Eds.), *Der islamische Fundamentalismus im 21. Jahrhundert. Analyse extremistischer Gruppen in westlichen Gesellschaften* (pp. 303–324). Springer VS.

Kolbe, A. R. (2019). Do Home-based Social Work Services Increase the Success of Programming to Prevent Violent Extremism: Evidence from a Small-scale Intervention in an Urban East African Population. *Clinical Research in Psychology, 2*(2), 1–6. https://asclepiusopen.com/clinical-research-in-psychology/volume-2-issue-2/5.pdf

Krafeld, F. J. (Ed.) (1992). *Cliquenorientierte Jugendarbeit. Grundlagen und Handlungsansaetze*. Juventa.

Krafeld, F. J. (Ed.) (1996). *Zuschlagen oder Zuhoeren. Jugendarbeit mit gewaltorientierten Jugendlichen*. Juventa.

Krafeld, F. J. (2016). *Jenseits von Erziehung. Begleiten und unterstützen statt erziehen und belehren*. Juventa.

Kubicek, B., & King, M. (2021). The Canada Centre and Countering Violent Extremism. In S. Carvin, T. Juneau, & C. Forcese (Eds.), *Top secret Canada: Understanding the Canadian intelligence and national security community* (pp. 181–198). University of Toronto Press.

Kurtz, L. F., Bagarozzi, D. A., & Pollane, L. P. (1984). Case Management in Mental Health. *Health & Social Work, 9*(3), 201–211. https://doi.org/10.1093/hsw/9.3.201

Leukefeld, C. G. (1990). Case management: A social work tradition. *Health & Social Work, 15*(3), 175–179. https://doi.org/10.1093/hsw/15.3.175

Leverson, J. (2017). Trauma-informed social work practice. *Social Work, 62*(2), 105–113. https://doi.org/10.1093/sw/swx001

Lösel, F., King, S., Bender, D., & Jugl, I. (2018). Protective factors against extremism and violent radicalization: A systematic review of research. *International Journal of Developmental Science, 12*(1–2), 89–102. https://doi.org/10.3233/DEV-170241

Marsden, S., & Lee, B. (2022). *Conceptualising protective factors: Strengths-based approaches [Report]*. Centre for Research and Evidence on Security Threats (CREST). Retrieved March 11, 2025, from https://crestresearch.ac.uk/resources/conceptualising-protective-factors-strengths-based-approaches/.

Marsden, S., & Lewis, J. (2021). *Trauma, adversity, and violent extremism [Report]*. Centre for Research and Evidence on Security Threats (CREST). Retrieved March 11, 2025, from https://crestresearch.ac.uk/resources/trauma-adversity-and-violent-extremism/.

Maylea, C., Makregiorgos, H., Martin, J., Alvarez-Vasquez, S., Dale, M., Hill, N., Johnson, B., Thomas, S., & Weller, P. (2020). Independent mental health advocacy: A model of social work advocacy? *Australian Social Work, 73*(3), 334–346. https://doi.org/10.1080/0312407X.2020.1725076

McKendrick, D., & Finch, J. (2017). 'Under heavy manners?': Social work, radicalisation, troubled families and non-linear war. *The British Journal of Social Work, 47*(2), 308–324. https://doi.org/10.1093/bjsw/bcv141

McKenzie, A., & O'Brien, D. (2024). The evolution of estimated time of arrival: The city of Toronto's CVE program. *Journal for Deradicalization, 39*, 94–128. https://journals.sfu.ca/jd/index.php/jd/article/view/911.

Moonshot. (2023). *Countering radicalization to violence in Ontario and Quebec: Canada's first online-offline interventions model*. Moonshot. Retrieved March 11, 2025, from https://moonshotteam.com/resource/countering-radicalization-to-violence-in-ontario-and-quebec/.

NASW. (2016). *NASW standards for social work practice in health care settings*. National Association of Social Workers. Retrieved March 11, 2025, from https://www.socialworkers.org/Practice/Practice-Standards-Guidelines.

NASW. (2021). *Code of ethics*. National Association of Social Workers. Retrieved March 11, 2025, from https://www.socialworkers.org.

Paré, D. (2014). Social justice and the word: Keeping diversity alive in therapeutic conversations. *Canadian Journal of Counselling and Psychotherapy, 48*(3), 206–217. https://cjc-rcc.ucalgary.ca/article/view/60996

PPN. (n.d.). *Who are we?* Prevention Practitioners Network (PPN). Retrieved March 11, 2025, from https://eradicatehatesummit.org/prevention-practitioners-network/.

Radvan, H. (2010). *Pädagogisches Handeln und Antisemitismus. Eine empirische Studie zu Beobachtungs- und Interventionsformen in der offenen Jugendarbeit*. Klinkhardt.

Regehr, C., & Glancy, G. (2014). Social work assessment in mental health. In C. Regehr & G. Glancy (Eds.), *Mental health social work practice in Canada* (2nd ed., pp. 74–96). Oxford University Press.

Roller, B., & Nelson, V. (1991). *The art of co-therapy: How therapists work together*. Guilford Press.

Sajid, M. S., Baikady, R., Sheng-Li, C., & Sakaguchi, H. (Eds.). (2020). *The Palgrave handbook of global social work education*. Palgrave Macmillan.

Saleebey, D. (1996). The Strengths Perspective in Social Work Practice: Extensions and Cautions. *Social Work, 41*(3), 296–305. https://doi.org/10.1093/sw/41.3.296

Scherr, A. (July 2001). Das Problem hat sich trotz Anstrengungen nicht verringert. Interview der Zeitschrift Christmon.

Sheafor, G., & Horejsi, C. R. (2006). *Techniques and guidelines for social work practice*. Pearson.

Solomon, B. B. (1987). Empowerment: Social work in oppressed communities. *Journal of Social Work Practice, 2*(4), 79–91. https://doi.org/10.1080/02650538708414984

Staller, K. M. (2019). Connecting the dots: What has terrorism got to do with social work? *Qualitative Social Work: Research and Practice, 18*(4), 557–561. https://doi.org/10.1177/1473325019857417

Stanley, T., & Guru, S. (2015). Childhood radicalisation risk: An emerging practice issue. *Practice: Social Work in Action, 27*(5), 353–366. https://doi.org/10.1080/09503153.2015.1053858

Stanley, T., Guru, S., & Coppock, V. (2017). A risky time for Muslim families: Professionalised counter-radicalisation networks. *Journal of Social Work Practice, 31*(4), 477–490. https://doi.org/10.1080/02650533.2017.1394829

Stanley, T., Guru, S., & Gupta, A. (2018). Working with PREVENT: Social work options for cases of 'Radicalisation Risk'. *Practice, 30*(2), 131–146. https://doi.org/10.1080/09503153.2017.1414176

Thomas, T., Thompson, D., & Karstedt, S. (2014). *Assessing the impact of circles of support and accountability on the reintegration of adults convicted of sexual offences in the community. Final Report*. Centre for Criminal Justice Studies, University of Leeds. Retrieved March 11, 2025, from https://essl.leeds.ac.uk/download/downloads/id/50/full_report.pdf.

Uhlmann, M. (2017). *Evaluation der Beratungsstelle "Radikalisierung": Abschlussbericht. (Forschungsbericht /Bundesamt für Migration und Flüchtlinge (BAMF) Forschungszentrum Migration, Integration und Asyl (FZ), 31)*. Bundesamt für Migration und Flüchtlinge (BAMF) Forschungszentrum Migration, Integration und Asyl (FZ).

Walkenhorst, D. (2022). Fragmentierung und Entkopplung. Warum im Feld der Distanzierungsarbeit kein systematischer Erfahrungs- und Wissensaustausch stattfindet—und was dagegen getan werden kann. *Unsere Jugend, 74*(4), 172–180.

Wolf, A. W., Goldfried, M. R., & Muran, J. C. (2013). *Transforming negative reactions to clients: From frustration to compassion*. American Psychological Association.

Wolf, A. W., Goldfried, M. R., & Muran, J. C. (2017). Therapist negative reactions: How to transform toxic experiences. In L. G. Castonguay & C. E. Hill (Eds.), *How and why are some therapists better than others? Understanding therapist effects* (pp. 175–192). American Psychological Association.

Yassine, L., & Briskman, L. (2019). Islamophobia and social work collusion. In D. Baines, B. Bennett, S. Goodwin, & M. Rawsthorne (Eds.), *Working across difference: Social work, social policy and social justice* (pp. 55–70). Red Globe Press.

Chapter 2
An Overview of Radicalization and Extremism Terminology and Theory

2.1 Introduction

Radicalization, hate, extremism, violent extremism, and terrorism have been and continue to be contested concepts. These concepts occupy entire bookshelves at local libraries and bookstores, while frequently being revised and critiqued by an array of disciplines and fields of study. Practitioners, scholars, and policymakers carry different assumptions about these terms. Each community applies its own mandates, cultural norms, and methods, shaping distinct views on how radicalization, hate, extremism, and terrorism interact with their organizational roles, professional expectations, and personal or intellectual values. Understanding these varied perspectives requires unpacking some of the evolution of the definitions underpinning these terminologies and their use, and understanding the complexity and interplay of professional, practical, and interdisciplinary contexts that condition them. In doing so, it becomes possible to critically evaluate their implications for social work policymaking, casework, case management, and academic inquiries into the character and consequences of radicalization and ideologically driven violence. Accordingly, this chapter emphasizes the importance of engaging with the multidimensional challenges posed by terrorism and extremism studies' theoretical frameworks, including some implications for social work practices in countering violent extremism (CVE) contexts.

2.2 Radicalization

Radicalization is conceptually fraught with politically weighted definitions, competing concepts, and misconceptions about the nature of extreme ideologically driven behavior and psychology. Although the etymological meaning of the prefix

D. Yuzva Clement et al., *Social Work and Countering Violent Extremism*, SpringerBriefs in Social Work, https://doi.org/10.1007/978-3-032-07086-9_2

to radicalization, namely, *radical*, is derived from the Latin word for *root* (*radix*), its meaning has changed considerably over time and in different contexts. For example, behaving *radically* was generally thought to be a politically or culturally reactionary or anomalous response to mainstream changes in social or economic structures, driven by either fringe emotional expression, controversial philosophies, social movement, or ethical action to provide an alternative ideological viewpoint or belief system (Neumann, 2013, 2017). Radicalism was in some situations found to be ethically necessary depending on perspective and the term's connotations at that moment. For example, radicalism was encouraged and considered the watchword for liberal reformers during the late nineteenth century, while during the early to middle twentieth century, Marxist revolutionaries were condemned as radicals and fanatics (Neumann, 2013, 2017). Unforeseen by their contemporaries, certain radical movements eventually inspired revolutionary, multi-generational changes in legal and social justice, such as the women's empowerment social movement which campaigned for their right to participate in political elections, or movements that once shifted the civil rights conversation in the United States, like Martin Luther King Jr. or Susan Brownell Anthony (Neumann, 2017). In this sense, *being radical* is not necessarily equal to the idea of unconstructive, undemocratic, and uncompromising ideological worldviews and extremist violence (Neumann, 2013; Tinnes, 2023). Due to this contrasting definitional history, a conceptual overview of the concept of radicalization is necessary to understand its interpretations in terrorism and extremism studies and consider its contemporary implications for social workers.

2.2.1 Radicalization: A Brief Overview of the Concept

From the 1960s until the 2020s, our scientific understanding of the primary cause of radicalization has changed significantly. Terrorism and extremism scholars historically pursued the *why question*, analyzing a terrorist's beliefs and behavior or a terrorist organization's activity at different levels, to devise insights about their intentions and ideological objectives in retrospect. At the individual level, scholars have investigated why some individuals may participate in organized ideological violence, and why others don't, as well as network dynamics, movement conduct, sociocultural conditions, and more recently, how social media platforms and other technologies make it easier to normalize and spread extremist views (Hutchinson et al., 2025; Hutchinson & Droogan, 2022). Researchers, policymakers, and practitioners sought to uncover *root causes* or *prime movers* that explained why some individuals (and not others) became radicalized and engaged in ideological violence (Veldhuis & Staun, 2009).

Early research on radicalization predominately focused on the psychology of "the radicalized." Here, the prospect of mental illness and psychological disorder as the causal precondition to extremism or terrorism was considered somewhat appealing because it effectively removed the possibility of a radicalized individual sharing the same moral rationality and conceivable reasonableness as in mainstream society (Baram, 2019). However, the association between mental illness and radicalization has received extensive challenge in recent years and, for that reason, is regarded as too narrow a focus for theory building and causality as a primary root cause (Corner et al., 2016, 2021; Neyroud et al., 2024).

Moving away from sole individual psychopathology, researchers then searched for reoccurring socioeconomic preconditions that were thought to provide the developmental or contextual foundations of the formally called *terrorist profile* (Corner et al., 2021; Horgan, 2008). However, the factors and circumstances found in the personal histories of terrorists, like those who executed Al Qaeda's September 11th 2001 terrorist attacks in the United States, feature a spectrum of socioeconomic class that are near irreducible to a single terrorist profile (Horgan, 2008). Similarly, regarding radicalization into Jihadist[1] violent extremism in the Canadian context, Dawson (2019, p. 159) found:

> Most glaringly, while some Western male recruits to jihadism, for example, have come from quite troubled backgrounds, with family issues, limited education, drug-abuse issues and criminality (...), others appear to have been model citizens, with happy family lives, university degrees, good jobs, spouses, and even children.

Accordingly, seeing as each terrorist's "profiles differ widely in race, age, social class, education, and family background," their preceding "motivations are equally diverse" (Vidino & Hughes, 2015, p. ix). Diversity in radicalization is now considered a canonical quality or characteristic of terrorism and extremism.

From 2001 to 2020, various theories, models, mechanisms, and metaphors emerged explaining why and how someone becomes radicalized (Kessler, 2016). For example, Crossett and Spitaletta (2010) identified 16 theories explaining the underlying cause of radicalization pathways, 12 psychological mechanisms explaining how a crowd, group, or individual undergoes the process of radicalization, and 16 risk factors within the literature that purported to support processes of radicalization. These conceptual approaches, grounded largely in psychosocial and

---

[1] The concept of "jihadism" is contested and problematic (Nash, 2021). Militant and terrorist groups such as Al Qaeda and ISIS have propagated *jihad* as a narrative of victimization and oppression by Western nations, using it to form transnational movements and justify violence. In contrast, researchers and Islamic studies scholars have repeatedly emphasized its theological and historical depth. Jihad has been debated and developed by Islamic scholarship and jurisprudence since the foundation of Islam, and scholars caution against equating it solely with violence, oppression, or war (Yuzva Clement, 2022). In terrorism and extremism studies, some researchers have used the concept of jihadism to frame the turn to extremism and terrorism as a plausible lens for reconstructing the pathways, lives, motives, and identities of recruits (Dawson, 2022). Roy, however, argued that Salafi-Jihadism represents a decultured expression of Islam, transforming the negative experiences of (mainly) European youth into a glorified, de-territorialized global community of like-minded individuals (Roy, 2013). Dawson critiqued Roy's approach, noting that Roy tends to dismiss the Islamic nature of Salafi-Jihadism by interpreting radicalization primarily through sociological and cultural lenses—as a youth aesthetic of violence—rather than through religious practice. Dawson disagreed with this reduction, arguing that Roy's observations are, in fact, compatible with the notion of lived religiosity, as practiced in complex, everyday lifeways (Dawson, 2022).

anthropological literatures of the time, sought to explain how individual, social, emotional, and cultural experiences were carried by cognitive mechanisms and shaped through enculturation (Bakker, 2006; Gartenstein-Ross et al., 2009; Hegghammer, 2006; Horgan, 2008, 2009; Sageman, 2008). This process, the above-mentioned authors argued, gradually shifted rationality and produced ideologically extreme viewpoints and behaviors.

Broadly speaking, radicalization researchers seek to understand what individuals think, how those individuals come to think what they think, and how individuals experience this thinking in ways that lead to certain extreme views and justifications for violent behaviors. In other words, it is essential to the concept radicalization, as Horgan (2019) remarked, that "people change" in their psychology, behavior, and relationships to such an extent that they are willing to become involved in violent extremism. For instance, Rousseau et al. (2020) suggested radicalization involves a pathway from a moderate perspective to an extreme, self-reinforcing, and even uncompromising viewpoint of social and political organization and meaning, wherein the person assumes an opposing position to demand commensurate or universal changes to society for the benefit of their beliefs and their ideological community.

2.2.2 *Evolution of Radicalization Models*

This section overviews predominant radicalization models developed in post-September 11th responses to terrorism. The first four models depict the arc or progression from politically benign citizen to ideologically driven violent extremist, namely: (1) the four-stage model, (2) the staircase model, (3) the group of guys theory, and (4) the process model. These models are all conditioned by their history and, subsequently, were primarily made to identify and assess cases of organizations and terrorist group activity in the context of religiously motivated violent extremism (Hirschfield et al., 2012; King & Taylor, 2011).

2.2.2.1 The Four-Stage Model

In early 2007, the New York Police Department's (NYPD) Intelligence Division conceptualized the Four-Stage Radicalization Model to gauge how individuals may undergo radicalization and how to pre-emptively address the prospect of violent extremism (Silber & Bhatt, 2007). This model emphasizes certain social, psychological, behavioral, or ideological factors at each stage (Silber, 2012). Although progression through these stages should not be considered linear, the framework offers valuable insight into the conditions that may underpin radicalization. Each stage represents four distinct changes to a person's social and psychological state when radicalization emerges: pre-radicalization in which an individual is disillusioned and searching (e.g., for recognition, cohesion, meaningfulness, sensuality);

self-identification wherein an individual detaches from their normal life and explores extremist material; indoctrination in which an individual assimilates into a network and mindset; and jihadization,[2] in which an individual commits or attempts extremist violence.

Critics of the NYPD's model raised important concerns about the model's limitations. The model oversimplifies a complex and highly individualized experience of radicalization by design and this simplification fails to account for the unique pathways to terrorism and motivations in individual cases that do not neatly match the four distinct stages. By focusing on four distinct stages, there are also risks of law enforcement inadvertently targeting individuals based on their perceived stage placement rather than actual behaviors or evidence of their intentions. However, the model functions as an analytical framework to be applied with discretion, not a guaranteed prediction of future radicalization.

2.2.2.2 Staircase to Terrorism

Another influential model for assessing radicalization to violence was the Staircase to Terrorism. This model was initially introduced by Fathali M. Moghaddam in 2005, conceptualizing an individual's change as analogous to traversing a social and psychological upward staircase. The staircase model is designed to illustrate a decision-making framework, where the person's exposure and reaction to certain personal and structural conditions at each stage may, or may not, nudge them toward subsequent stages or steps of commitment, bringing them closer to legitimizing ideological violence (Moghaddam, 2005; Vermeulen & Visser, 2021). The staircase metaphor is analogous to some classical developmental stage theories, where individuals can ascend or descend the *steps*, but progression to higher levels requires the completion of the preceding steps with each successive series of processes (or *floors*) representing the individual's intensifying radicalization to violence (Lygre et al., 2011). While this model has undergone considerable revision since its conception (Lygre et al., 2011; Paniagua, 2005), the stages generally consist of six stages in which an individual experiences deprivation and injustice; ideologically informed sense of self in relation to injustice; belief that conventional methods of redress are impossible; adopt an uncompromising us-versus-them worldview; disengage from societal morals and dehumanize the perceived enemy; preparing for violence; disable inhibitions and operationalize violence (Baram, 2019; Hirschfield et al., 2012; King & Taylor, 2011; Moghaddam, 2005; Moghadam, 2006).

Despite its impressive influence in the CVE sphere, the staircase model also faces significant criticism for oversimplification and failing to account for uniqueness and the non-linear nature of radicalization. Critics argued that the model

[2] As discussed, the usage of terminology such as "jihadization," as employed in the NYPD's four-stage model of radicalization, is problematic. It reflects a reductive and Islam-centric framing that risks conflating religious belief with violent extremism, reinforcing bias, othering, and contributing to the securitization of Muslim communities (Nash, 2021).

underemphasizes contextual factors, implying a one-way journey, potentially justifying premature profiling, and leading to ineffective interventions. This aligns with additional literature reviews suggesting radicalization research has predominantly focused on the individual event, rather than the person themselves, and until recently, online–offline environments where the person developed their views (Bouhana, 2019; Gill et al., 2015; Hutchinson, 2023). The model's geographic origins may also reflect Western-centric views, possibly overlooking nuances in non-Western contexts. Furthermore, one critical oversight in how these processes are embedded in digital media infrastructure includes algorithmic curation and encrypted peer validation which can often propel individuals past multiple "floors" while unseen. This critique is not exclusive to the staircase model; the aforementioned four stage radicalization model also proposed a linear progression through successive stages that implies radicalization is likely to lead to violence. However, current research has transitioned away from one coherent model and understands radicalization more so as a multidimensional, context-specific, and non-linear phenomenon (Hutchinson, 2023; McCauley & Moskalenko, 2017).

2.2.2.3 Group of Guys Theory

Drawing on his assessment of media sources and hundreds of Al Qaeda-affiliated terrorism and extremism cases, Marc Sageman (2008) developed the Group of Guys Theory of radicalization. This model emphasizes the predominant role of personal, social, and gender dynamics, underscoring the influential experiences that groups of younger males have while embedded in ideological support networks. According to Sageman (2008, p. 37), these groups are often composed of individuals that

> "do not even adhere to the most austere and dogmatic tenets of radical ideologies, but instead, consisted of homegrown wannabes—self-recruited, without leadership, and globally connected through the Internet. They are young people seeking thrills and a sense of significance and belonging in their lives," merging "their lack of structure and organizing principles" with a yearning for quests, recognition, and purpose.

These groups are typically composed of strong social ties, often existing through friendships, kinship, or shared experiences, creating a foundational channel for disseminating radical ideas without immediate skepticism.

Crucially, Sageman highlighted how the group dynamic fosters an intense sense of belonging and identity transformation. The insularity of these groups amplifies their influence, as members can perceive themselves as part of a noble mission, which serves to validate their actions, strengthen their commitment to the group's identity, and reframes their personal grievances and ambitions within the group's goals, moral superiority, and ideological justifications. Rather than an isolated cognitive journey, Sageman's group of guys model highlights interpersonal bonds and group dynamics as catalyzing the process of radicalization, accentuating the influence from in-person group dynamics in shaping extremist psychology and behavior. Critique of this model will follow the below Process Model explanation, as both models take a similar approach to account for complexity and thus find themselves in similar shortcomings.

2.2.2.4 The Process Model

The Process Model is based on a simple yet important view: everyone's pathway to radicalization and violence is *different*. The journey to violent extremism is highly individualized and complex, influenced by a wide range of psychological, social, and environmental factors. Accordingly, John Horgan's (2014) Process Model outlines a sequential and yet, non-deterministic pathway that is composed of three major segments to radicalization and violence: Involvement, Engagement, and Disengagement. Based on his examination of Al Qaeda members prosecuted for terrorism in America, Horgan (2014) outlined their arc of radicalization and various factors that may have contributed to each individual's organizational role, categorizing their role as either: active participant, aspirant, facilitator, trained aspirant, or ideologue. These categories already illustrate the variety of ways individuals can radicalize to engage in terrorist activity, while reflecting the diversity of processes that led them there. Furthermore, Horgan's (2014, p. 81) model is empirically grounded in the observation that all violent extremists assessed were "psychologically extremely heterogeneous," proposing that "dissimilarity is a very pervasive theme when we look to compare profiles of who becomes involved in terrorism." Subsequently, the Process Model assumes a far more flexible, non-linear, multivariate understanding of radicalization and violence. In other words, two principles to the process model are as follows: the recognition of individuals' psychological and behavioral diversity, and that radicalization is a multivariate process shaped by unique, personal circumstances and their interaction with them over time.

Such flexibility is one of the model's greatest strengths. It encompasses numerous influences, including ideological, social, emotional, and situational factors without oversimplifying or reducing radicalization to a single cause or origin. Importantly, it also highlights the potential for concurrent pathways to deradicalization and disengagement, showing that individuals can and do leave extremist pathways, whether it be through personal choice, external intervention, or disillusionment. Furthermore, there is no fixed link between ideological violence and the final phase of radicalization. Different ideologies and behaviors may emerge at various stages for some individuals, not appear at all for others, or gradually escalate (i.e., from subtle interpersonal intimidation to full commitment to extremist violence). In prioritizing complexity or individuality, the Process Model provides a comprehensive and adaptable framework for radicalization.

Even more constructive theories—such as Sageman's Group of Guys theory and Horgan's Process Model—have not escaped criticism. Both rely heavily on the scholar or practitioner's assessment of an individual's complex journey, including the multitude of contextual factors and the developmental milieu from which they emerge (Borum, 2011b). These assessments, however, often depend on the limited evidence available to an individual researcher, which can constrain the depth and reliability of analysis. Moreover, these models struggle to account for virtual and technological influences, particularly when individuals are not overtly active or vocal online. Digital media environments allow individuals to support extremist groups or terrorist organizations without formal membership or offline commitments, complicating the detection of roles and stages.

2.2.3 General Critiques of Post-9/11 Radicalization Models

While it is important to highlight the immense contributions that these radicalization models have made, there are worthwhile critiques to highlight, too. For one, the models were developed to understand radicalization primarily within the context of religiously motivated violent extremism in the decade following the terrorist attacks of September 11th 2001. Some, therefore, consider the term *radicalization* to be scientifically questionable because it incorrectly implies that radical beliefs are the prime mover or precursor to extremism and terrorism, and it amassed significant political baggage from the U.S.' declarations in the War on Terror (Awan et al., 2012; Borum, 2011a; Silva, 2018). Against this backdrop, some adjacent concepts including *Islamism* or *Jihadism* are widely critiqued as discussed earlier, and we share this criticism, because they place linguistic and theoretical assumptions on the religion of Islam and of religiosity as particularly influential, if not determinant, factors in radicalization. The normalization of such assumptions about the role of religion is viewed by researchers as having contributed to the widespread securitization of Muslim communities in varied Western democratic countries due to the "jihadi-centric threat narrative, which influenced what constituted terrorism" (Nash, 2021, p. 4). It is essential for social workers engaged in CVE to remain critically aware of the sociohistorical and geopolitical contexts in which concepts like radicalization were coined. This awareness enables social workers to approach clients more ethically and effectively, ensuring that interventions are culturally sensitive, evidence-based, and up to date (Borum, 2011a, 2011b; Gill et al., 2015; Meleagrou-Hitchens et al., 2017; Odag et al., 2019; Scrivens, 2020; Schuurman, 2020).

As aforementioned, how and when someone undergoes radicalizing changes is inherently difficult to pinpoint because it is fundamentally an outcome of *multifinality*: a single factor leads to multiple behavioral outcomes; and *equifinality*: where the same outcome can manifest from multiple factors or a combination of factors (Horgan, 2019; Khalil et al., 2019). This, in other words, *problem of specificity* is the (almost) quixotic empirical challenge for the field to overcome (Biene & Junk, 2017; Dawson, 2019; Neumann, 2013; Rousseau et al., 2020). Regardless, the stage-based frameworks have been instrumental in progressing the methodological and empirical sophistication of extremism and terrorism studies, highlighting sequential aspects of radicalization as key milestones along the way, and stressing the importance of non-linear, environmental-dependent, highly complex, and recursive characteristics of radicalization pathways in their wake.

2.2.4 Dynamic Models of Radicalization

Dynamic models of radicalization were introduced to incorporate thinking around the problem of specificity and non-ideological motivators. McCauley and Moskalenko (2008) initially proposed the Pyramid to Radicalization to show how terrorists form a very small subset of a population that shares a similar ideology and grievance. They later updated their model to respond to the criticism that the overwhelming majority of people who hold violent beliefs toward themselves or others never act on them, while others who do not seem as embedded in a terrorist ideology or group can still commit violence. The evolved Two Pyramids Model (McCauley & Moskalenko, 2017) aims to capture two theoretically distinct groups of people: those who progress to extremist violence because of their belief system (e.g., full endorsement of an extremist ideology) and those who progress to extremist violence for other reasons (e.g., love, social status in peer group, desire for violence). The strength of this improved model is recognizing the importance that non-ideological factors can play in someone's radicalization pathway.

Another theory that moved away from the phased approach is the Radicalization Puzzle (Hafez & Mullins, 2015). In this approach, analysts are encouraged to not assume progression between states but to look for discrete risk factors that all fit together to make sense of each individual case. This model focused on four types of factors: grievances which include economic marginalization or other types of injustice; networks of extremist people; ideologies that legitimize violence toward outgroups; and enabling environments that propel individuals to violence. The Radicalization Puzzle invites to view each "puzzle piece" both individually and as part of its contribution to the whole of a person's radicalization. The goal in doing this is to avoid the mistake of grouping together people simply because they share an identifying trait, such as belonging to a certain social group.

Both models were designed to focus on the so-called homegrown Islamist terrorism in Western contexts which limits the discourse and subject matter available to them. In 2019, Khalil et al. (2019) introduced the two-dimensional *Attitudes-Behavior Corrective (ABC) Model*: a dynamic rather than a phase or process model of radicalization which shifts away from an ideologically or religiously focused theory and highlights the probability that some individuals participate in violent extremism and do not necessarily attribute the motivation behind their actions to an extremist ideology. Subsequently, other motivating or dynamic factors including that of economic gains, social status, adventure seeking, among many others, can also be motivational drivers behind an individual's own participation in violent extremism. Simply put, this model, and adjoining research, asks what function (e.g., social, identity-formation) extremist ideology or group belonging plays in someone's radicalization trajectory. As a dynamic model, it proposes that individuals might change their attitudes and behaviors over time, resulting in a near infinite number of trajectories in radicalization. Accordingly, Khalil et al. (2019) then applied the idea of equifinality and differentiated between structural motivators (e.g., contextual factors), individual factors (e.g., psychosocial and material incentives), and enabling factors (e.g., mentors, online communities, and social networks) that can propel individuals toward extremist attitudes or behaviors (Khalil et al., 2019; McCauley, 2020; Schuurman et al., 2018).[3]

---

[3] McCauley (2020) compared the Two-Pyramid and ABC Models, noting similarities and differences, especially regarding structural drivers of extremism. He critiqued Khalil's use of Rational Choice Theory, while Khalil argued self-interest still motivates group-aligned actions. Others chal-

By moving beyond ideologically focused frameworks, dynamic models shed light on the particular risk factors that contribute to radicalization, as well as protective factors that keep clients and communities safe. By further building upon these dimensional models, social work can better understand and intervene in how individuals become susceptible to extremist ideologies, communities, and aesthetics, and design tailored and ethical intervention and prevention strategies.

2.2.5 Dimensions of Radicalization and Current Trends

Contemporary research continues to develop and empirically test various dimensions of radicalization, recognizing its complexity and multifaceted nature. As early as the 1980s, Sherry Cable et al. (1988) argued that rather than seeking a single explanatory model, analysts should acknowledge the existence of multiple models, each applicable under different conditions. Over time, radicalization research has progressively incorporated multidimensional approaches that align with more developmental, constructivist, and individualist perspectives on how radicalization occurs (Borum, 2011a, 2011b). Rather than being understood as a fixed outcome, radicalization is now widely viewed as an iterative and self-reinforcing process, shaped by the dynamic interplay between individuals, ideologies, and relationships, gradually shifting people toward extreme beliefs and behaviors (McCormick, 2003). As proposed by abovementioned dynamic models of radicalization, this perspective recognizes that individuals may not follow a linear trajectory but instead move fluidly between stages of radicalization across different systems and social contexts (Carthy & Schuurman, 2024). For example, with regard to adverse childhood experiences (ACE), Carthy and Schuurman (2024) used a statistical analysis, continuum-based approach to examine how varying degrees of early-life adversity had contributed to varied pathways toward radicalization. Carthy and Schuurman (2024) found those who were radicalized and subsequently became involved in terrorist violence were more likely to have experienced ACEs than those who radicalized but did not engage in violence. Furthermore, it was found that the relationship between ACEs and involvement in terrorist violence was significant for those who abandoned education during radicalization, while time spent in education was found to act as a protective factor in this relationship between ACEs and the role of school education with regard to radicalization processes (Carthy & Schuurman, 2024). This points, as discussed earlier, to radicalization as a non-linear phenomenon of equifinality that is not dependent on a single causal factor (Carthy & Schuurman, 2024; Rousseau et al., 2020).

The notions of *grievance-fueled violence* and *targeted violence* have also recently received scholarly attention because they propose to understand the underlying

---

lenged the "lone-actor" concept, emphasizing social ties in radicalization (Khalil et al., 2020; Schuurman et al., 2018).

motivations and risk factors of different violent offenders as well as their interrelations, such as terrorists, mass murderers, hate crime offenders, and perpetrators of fatal family violence (Alberda et al., 2022; Corner et al., 2023; Vergani & Hutchinson, 2024). In general terms, Sizoo et al. (2022) suggested grievance is an unfolding experience that involves sense-making through regulation of one's interaction with the social environment. Subsequently, grievance involves both implicit negative affect (sense-making) and the perceived injustice inflicted by another (interpersonal relatedness) in ways that can lead to avoidance or violent behavior (Sizoo et al., 2022).

Another notable trend is engagement in or perpetration of *nihilistic violence*. This form of violence is understood as a hybridized blend of apocalyptic thinking and antisocial and misanthropic practices, subcultures, and behaviors. It is driven not primarily by ideology or political goals, but by a sense of meaninglessness or despair. While some nihilistic online spaces can be nonviolent, research has identified several violent groups and chat forums, such as the so-called *Com* network and groups like *764*, that convene, blend, propagate, coerce, and glorify violence. This includes mass violence, self-harm and suicide, animal abuse, gender-based violence and sexual violence, child abuse, and violent extremism. These spaces tend to normalize, desensitize, and fetishize violence trough exploitation, grooming, and victimization of often young and vulnerable users (Argentino et al., 2024; Purdue, 2022).

There is particular concern over the online radicalization of transitional aged youth (TAY). This period of life, from approximately 16 to 24 years (Chan & Derenne, 2021) represents an existential bridge for many young people in several ways. For instance, they are engaged in the developmental tasks of moving toward self-sufficiency, pursuing (post-secondary) education and employment, and negotiating intimate and romantic relationships. They are often individuating from their families of origin, becoming more concerned with peer group validation as well as finding a social group, and for some transitioning out of child welfare programming. In short, their adult agency is emerging and it will be used to form a new worldview. This period of life is also associated with significant risks. TAY are overrepresented in mental health challenges, substance misuse, and suicide (Chan & Derenne, 2021; MacKinnon & Colman, 2016). Also of note, while the risks are increased during this transitional period, TAY do not engage in commensurate help-seeking behaviors and are increasingly suffering in isolation from professional helpers or their closest friends, caregivers, and family (Stunden et al., 2020). In Australia, Canada, New Zealand, the United Kingdom, and the United States, law enforcement and security agencies have recently reported that there is a growing trend of TAY involvement in online extremism forums (Royal Canadian Mounted Police, 2024). As such, there is particular interest in understanding why extremist worldviews and content are attractive to children, teenagers, and emerging adults that are seeking to establish a place for themselves in the world (*see* Chap. 4).

2.2.5.1 Risk Factors to Radicalization

There are numerous risk and protective factors said to perpetuate and mitigate radicalization processes. Because factors (e.g., employment, education, or emotional regulation, and so on) are distributed in the wider population, the listing of factors as constructive variables in a checklist of radicalization is misleading and could likely lead to discrimination and stigmatization through false positives. Nonetheless, risk factors remain necessary to compartmentalize and make assessments of the individual's character, expression of their lifestyle, the nature of their social relations and societal embeddedness, or other factors yet unaccounted for (Lösel et al., 2018). For instance, it is important to understand what conditional factors may prove significant in one person's journey toward radicalization; however, in line with equifinality and multifinality, those conditional factors may be entirely insignificant in another's journey (Wolfowicz et al., 2021). When undertaking risk assessment, practitioners must acknowledge when certain factors could accumulate or interact with each other to increase or decrease the likelihood of the person pursuing ideological violence (Carthy & Schuurman, 2024). In Wolfowicz et al.'s (2021) systematic evidence review of risk and protective factors, cognitive, behavioral, as well as sociodemographic factors were deemed significant contributors, while another review suggested that offenders emerged from a diversity of socioeconomic backgrounds (middle- or upper-class) (Lösel et al., 2018; Wolfowicz et al., 2021).

Experiential and attitudinal factors, such as perceived strain, grievances, and relative deprivation also emerged as pivotal influences (Wolfowicz et al., 2021). A hostile sociopolitical context, coupled with prolonged stress and feelings of exclusion, may exacerbate both the individual's and the community's ideological grievances. These experiences often lead to social isolation and a diminished sense of identity, creating vulnerabilities that extremist recruiters readily exploit. Such feelings of insignificance, frequently stemming from discrimination, unemployment, or other adverse events, make cognitive openings such as selective empathy, uncompromising us-versus-them thinking, and out-group enmity more likely to occur and are at times described as a *quest for significance* (Wolfowicz et al., 2021). Individuals that are allured by adventure, social recognition, lack of personal meaning, and cultural validation are vulnerable to the psychological appeals of radicalizing views, with thrill-seeking and low self-control performing an important role, particularly for individuals harboring trauma, depression, suicidality, and emotional dysregulation (Carthy & Schuurman, 2024; Sarma et al., 2022; Wolfowicz et al., 2021). Criminogenic factors stress that social learning and reinforcement occur in these psychosocial environments, wherein deviant peer groups, familial networks, and online extremist communities further incentivize and strengthen extremist views, attitudes, or behaviors. Additionally, criminological histories, prior incarceration or criminal justice involvement (*see* Chap. 4), and unemployment are said to exacerbate vulnerabilities to radicalization, particularly for those already participating in (online) ideological support networks (Wolfowicz et al., 2021).

Furthermore, mental health issues may contribute to violent radicalization as dynamic or enabling risk factors (CPN-PREV, 2025; McKenzie & O'Brien, 2024;

Rousseau et al., 2022). While there is no causality between mental health and violent radicalization, emerging data in Canada revealed that extremist clients who participated in psychosocial CVE intervention programs struggled with a broad range of mental health conditions or challenges (alongside other risk factors and unmet needs, e.g., family conflict, social isolation) such as traumatic stress, depression, and mood and anxiety disorders. Some clients had also been diagnosed with a neurodevelopmental disorder such as autism spectrum disorder or attention-deficit/hyperactivity disorder (McKenzie & O'Brien, 2024; Rousseau et al., 2022). Rousseau et al. (2022) remind us that psychosocial CVE interventions and mental health services, as well as training and capacity building for frontline professionals, are important institutions and services to address these underlying vulnerabilities and to ensure individual and public safety.

Understanding the interplay of factors is important for developing holistic CVE interventions and prevention strategies that address radicalization to violence. Social workers should be cognizant of balancing the need to remain informed about such factors, while also remaining flexible, unassuming, and collaborative to understand the specific and unique influence that these factors have on clients. Vulnerability is not confined to ideology, individual traits, nor isolated contexts. Rather, it arises from dynamic and distributed systematic interactions within internal, personal, community, and macropolitical settings including in online contexts. Accumulated risk factors, combined with a lack of protective factors, can push individuals toward radicalization, or conversely, when a person has an abundance of protective factors and limited risk factors, this presupposes the individual harbors resilience and can foster social and psychological stability when necessary. However, protective factors are not merely the inverse of risk factors, and neither factor is guaranteed to have effect (Lösel et al., 2018). For example, specific factors such as the adherence to law and authority, sustained employment, and strong social relationship all moderate the effects of radicalization generally speaking, while health issues or empathy toward others can also play unexpected roles in discouraging violence. Therefore, interpersonal approaches to addressing radicalization must recognize both the cumulative and circumstantial nature of risk factors and protective factors in someone's experience of becoming radicalized, acknowledging the context-specificity of risk and protective factors. Social workers are uniquely well-positioned to intervene across this multitude of risk and protective factors, given their holistic, person-in-environment perspective and their training in addressing complex social, psychological, and structural issues.

As well, recent research has found commonalities and differences between risk factors for violent radicalization and other forms of violence. Indeed, while certain risk factors and sources of influence are specific to extremist violence, such as online exposure and engagement within extremist milieus and extreme forms of attitudes, there are several risk and protective factors shared *between* violent extremism and other forms of violence (CPN-PREV, 2025). These include prior criminal history, deviant peers, being younger, adverse childhood experiences, low parental involvement in childhood, unemployment and low educational attainment, proneness to anger and hostility (CPN-PREV, 2025). This research also found that other risk factors or domains, commonly accounted for in other forms of violence, are largely neglected in violent extremism research and assessment, including substance abuse, certain personality disorders (e.g., antisocial, borderline), prior engagement in violence, and hypermasculinity/hostile masculinity (CPN-PREV, 2025). Consequently, this research called for greater attention of criminogenic risk factors studied in other fields as well as for prevention efforts grounded in psychosocial interventions and social reintegration beyond a sole focus on ideology.

2.3 Hate, Extremism, Violent Extremism, and Terrorism

In the following sections, we overview the concepts hate, extremism, violent extremism, and terrorism, including the interoperability between distinct yet ideologically overlapping extremist communities (e.g., right-wing extremism[4] and incel or involuntary celibate communities). Following this, we summarize the practical and theoretical implications of these conceptualizations for social workers, questioning the way these terms may impact social work's approach to CVE.

2.3.1 Hate and Hate Crimes

Emotions are fundamental to human cognition and behavior. They are not irrational forces to be suppressed, but essential components of how we interpret the world, make decisions, and relate to others. Emotions help us prioritize what matters, signal threats or opportunities, and motivate action. While emotions like empathy and compassion can foster social cohesion, others—such as fear, resentment, and humiliation—can contribute to division and violence. Among these, hate stands out as a particularly enduring and identity-focused emotion. Hate is an emotional state of enmity or malice directed at individuals, groups, or communities based on characteristics such as ethnicity, religion, gender identity, or sexual orientation (Brown,

[4] In general terms, far-right or right-wing extremism encompasses a broad spectrum of views, agendas, and communities advocating forms of nativism, white supremacy, authoritarianism, social inequality, neo-Nazism, accelerationism, Antisemitism, Islamophobia, misogyny, male supremacism, and anti-2SLGBTQI+ sentiment, with strategic crossovers in populist or conspiratorial politics. While some participants operate within democratic systems ("radical right"), others reject democratic legitimacy entirely ("extreme right"), justifying violence as a means of accelerating systemic collapse (Ravndal & Bjørgo, 2018). In contrast, far-left movements and violent extremist groups such as the Red Army Faction, the Weather Underground, and Italy's Red Brigades engaged in targeted political violence, including assassinations, sabotage, and attacks on government and corporate infrastructure. While far-left violence has declined in frequency and severity compared to the far-right in recent decades, extremist actors remain active in militant networks, often with decentralized structures and varying thresholds for violence (Ravndal & Bjørgo, 2018).

2017). Unlike fleeting emotions like anger, hate is enduring—*it targets people for who they are,* not what they do (Deloughery et al., 2012; Vergani & Hutchinson, 2024). This emotional disposition can serve as a precursor to both hate crimes and violent extremism, acting as a psychological and ideological fuel for violence. Hate speech refers to expressions that vilify or incite hatred against a group, often with the intent to dehumanize and inspire harm or reinforce social hierarchies. While not always criminal, hate speech contributes to a broader ecosystem of normalization and justification for violence (Vergani & Hutchinson, 2024)—and, as research has found, hateful and dehumanizing rhetoric is statistically likely to lead to violent outcomes (Angove, 2024).

Hate crimes are criminal acts—such as assault, vandalism, or murder—motivated by bias or prejudice against a protected characteristic. While they are often spontaneous and unplanned, they can also be premeditated and deliberately targeted. Hate crimes are frequently described as "downward crimes," where perpetrators from dominant social groups target marginalized communities, reinforcing existing power imbalances (Deloughery et al., 2012). In contrast, violent extremism involves ideologically motivated violence aimed at achieving political, religious, ideological, or social objectives. These acts are typically premeditated, carried out by individuals or groups with a shared belief system, and often target institutions or symbols of perceived oppression. However, recent research suggested that factors beyond extremist ideology can drive individuals toward violent extremism, with radicalization often rooted in highly individualized and personalized grievances, as well as the hybridization of different extremist milieus (Gartenstein-Ross & Plant, 2023; Khalil et al., 2019). Violent extremism is sometimes described as "upward," directed against democracy writ large and those seen as part of a dominant or hegemonic system (Deloughery et al., 2012). Yet, hate crimes can also be understood as "upward" in their broader societal impact: by attacking the dignity, safety, and rights of targeted individuals, they also strike at the foundational values of equality, inclusion, and human rights that underpin democratic societies (Mills et al., 2015). Despite their theoretical distinctions, hate crimes and violent extremism often overlap conceptually and practically. Both are *crimes of message*, aimed at intimidating not only the immediate victim but also a broader community. As a result, the terms are sometimes used interchangeably in practice, blurring the clear-cut distinctions emphasized by researchers.

Many jurisdictions have legal definitions of hate crimes, which typically include a range of specific offences when motivated by bias against characteristics like race, religion, national origin, sexual orientation, gender identity, or disability. These laws vary across countries and regions, with some offering enhanced penalties for bias-motivated crimes. Several studies have shown that victims of hate crimes suffer greater psychological harm than victims of comparable non-bias crimes. These harms include increased levels of depression, anxiety, anger, stress, and fear of future victimization. Despite their impact, hate crimes are widely underreported, often due to fear of retaliation, lack of trust in authorities, or uncertainty about whether the incident qualifies as a hate crime. While hate crime and violent extremism are distinct concepts, they exist on a continuum of bias-motivated harm, with hate as a common emotional foundation (Brown, 2017; Deloughery et al., 2012).

2.3.2 *Extremism*

Extremism is considered an intellectual position, a set of belief systems, and an action orientation encompassing specific behaviors and psychological dispositions. It operates in direct opposition to the fundamental political and cultural values of mainstream society, particularly democratic principles and practices as well as human rights (Neumann, 2017). This conceptualization allows researchers to differentiate extremism from radical perspectives and behaviors. Radicalism, while it may involve the adoption of dangerous beliefs, does not discard democratic norms or values necessarily. Radical views can co-exist within a legitimate political framework and may aim to reform or strengthen societal structures rather than dismantle them entirely. Radicalization as a pathway or process involves the progressive adoption of beliefs, experiences, or ideological exposure that may or may not lead to violence. In contrast, extremism is characterized by its dogmatic, uncompromising, and anti-democratic nature, rejecting the possibility of a peaceful coexistence with opposing views or priorities. Furthermore, extremism denotes a fixed ideological stance. Extremists adhere to the worldviews that see no middle ground and impose no limitations on their or their communities' means to achieve ideological objectives (Hutchinson, 2024; Schuurman & Taylor, 2018). Extremists are therefore marked by their psychological rigidity and the ideological hostility that extends beyond hate and intellectual disagreement into active dehumanization or aggression toward their perceived political, social, or cultural opponents. While extremism provides the ideological foundations for violent actions, not all extremists engage in violence. Violent extremism or terrorism specifically refers to the usage and justification of violence or threats of violence to achieve ideological objectives or a political cause (Schuurman & Taylor, 2018).

2.3.2.1 Salad-Bar Extremism

Salad-bar extremism refers to the personalized and unorthodox blend of extremist belief systems by groups or individuals. Unlike traditional extremist groups or individuals that adhered to distinct and relatively singular ideological frameworks, the notion of salad-bar extremism involves the ad-hoc exercise of *cherry-picking* elements from disparate ideological communities to construct tailor-made, adaptable, and eccentric extremist worldviews (Organization for the Prevention of Violence, 2022). The term was originally coined to describe a subset of American right-wing extremists, and since gained broader relevance across the global extremist threat landscape. For instance, in Canada, the Organization for the Prevention of Violence identified a critical shift within right-wing extremist ideologies.

Traditional boundaries between white supremacy, anti-government, and anti-authority extremism, and extreme misogyny blurred, resulting in a more nebulous ideological bricolage, where individuals selectively combined portions of these ideologies to create bespoke belief systems that resonated with their personal grievances and ambitions (Gartenstein-Ross & Plant, 2023; Organization for the Prevention of Violence, 2022).

For example, certain ideological and emotional commonalties in far-right and incel[5] communities have facilitated the cross-pollination and combination of beliefs online. Wilson (2020, p. 2) found the concept of "white genocide" to be a foundational, mutually reinforcing schema in white supremacy and misogynistic extremism, represented at times as the demand for violent extremism as retribution for "the damage caused by feminism, women's economic and sexual independence, miscegenation (interracial sexual relations), and falling birth rates." White supremacy and misogyny feature cultural mechanisms for nostalgia and commemoration, including the idealization of previous violent extremists, the revitalization of periods in history, such as Nazi Germany (Droogan & Hutchinson, 2024; Hutchinson et al., 2025; Kelly & Aunspach, 2020; O'Donnell & Shor, 2022; Wilson, 2020). This is not to suggest communities where far-right or incel discussions occur are ideologically the same, or convergent phenomena in all cases (Cottee, 2021; Gentry, 2022; Jackson, 2019). Numerous cases have shown that men have committed acts of mass violence in response to gendered grievances, often accelerated through online platforms. In some instances, these grievances have been framed ideologically—as seen in Canada's conviction of an incel-affiliated perpetrator under terrorism laws. Different online hate networks frequently celebrate such attacks, glorify the perpetrators, and encourage further harm by reframing personal frustrations into a broader narrative of symbolic status, collective injustice, and perceived victimhood (Tran, 2025).

In this sense, extremists have recently demonstrated only a superficial or inconsistent commitment to any specific ideological framework, suggesting their experience of radicalization may be driven as much by a search for personal meaning, belonging, or adventure as by particular ideological convictions (Schuurman, 2020). This shift necessitates a re-evaluation of existing CVE frames to account for the role of personalization. For instance, traditional approaches too-often relied on clear and categorical ideological markers, but the eclectic nature of salad-bar extremism makes it difficult to address it effectively. Instead, researchers emphasized the importance of conceptually characterizing an individual's or community's

[5] Involuntary celibate (incels) online communities form part of the broader misogynistic "manosphere." Incel ideologies blend toxic masculinity, nihilism, and violent misogyny with extremist worldviews, including white supremacy and eugenics. By referring to the so-called black pill and other such ideological frameworks, incels describe themselves as unable to form romantic or sexual relationships, and are united by experiences of exclusion, humiliation, and certain beliefs about unjust social hierarchies privileging women's sexual choice and exacerbating their perceived social and biological inferiority (Gheorghe & Yuzva Clement, 2023). Although ideologically fragmented, incel communities have been implicated in gender-based violence, violent extremism, and the aesthetic and ideological glorification of violent actors, including far-right and jihadist perpetrators who espouse rigid gender hierarchies and targeted violence (Gheorghe & Yuzva Clement, 2023).

ideological position with nuance and specificity to mitigate the risks of over-generalization and analytical inaccuracy (Gartenstein-Ross & Plant, 2023; Ravndal & Bjørgo, 2018). This approach recognizes the diversity within broader extremist movements, acknowledging that ideologies are shaped by a range of social, political, and psychological factors. For instance, the Centre for the Prevention of Radicalization Leading to Violence (2024) describes five overarching ideological dimensions that extremists commonly integrate to shape their belief systems: environmental concerns; spiritual or religious mobilization; community belonging; gender dynamics[6]; and individual freedoms. A few governments have also discontinued the use of terms like far-right and right-wing terrorism, substituting them with updated categories (Hutchinson, 2024). Technologies like social networking are thought to facilitate and accelerate phenomena such as salad-bar extremism, enabling users to sample and merge diverse ideologies in quick succession (Davey & Ebner, 2017; Gartenstein-Ross & Blackman, 2019). Examining the characteristics and implications of salad-bar extremism will enable practitioners in social work to understand and address how contemporary extremist communities evolve and express themselves in increasingly hybridized manner.

2.3.3 Violent Extremism

The concept of violent extremism underscores the violent aspects or outcomes of extremism, encompassing a range of violent behaviors that include physical and psychological actions that are primarily motivated by an extreme ideological, and as discussed above, often hybridized, mentality (Berger, 2018; Hutchinson, 2024; Neumann, 2017). Violent extremism is considered the deliberate use of force or violence to advance one (or more) ideological objectives that advocate for racial, cultural, political, and/or religious supremacy and are fundamentally opposed to mainstream societal values, such as liberalism, democracy, and human rights (Neumann, 2013). Violent extremism has encompassed both physical and

[6] Gender is a significant motivational factor influencing individuals to join extremist groups and online forums. Gender identity and gender relations form a core part of many extremist ideologies, often framed as gendered empowerment rooted in patriarchal norms and rigid stereotypes. A common narrative within these ideologies is the perception that one's gender is under threat—socially, culturally, or politically—which can fuel a desire to reclaim power or restore status. These narratives can be particularly appealing as they offer a sense of purpose, belonging, clarity, or power within a structured worldview. In contrast, contemporary understandings of gender are becoming increasingly inclusive and fluid, challenging traditional binaries and expanding the spectrum of identity and expression. For some, these shifts are perceived as destabilizing or threatening to established social orders, further reinforcing extremist appeals to restore "traditional" gender roles. Regardless of gender, individuals can occupy both violent and non-violent roles within extremist or terrorist groups, organizations, and digital networks. Understanding these gendered dimensions is essential for developing more effective prevention and intervention strategies (Hutchinson et al., 2025).

psychological force, including actions that support the use of violence, such as spreading narratives, recruiting members, traveling abroad to join violent movements, and providing financial, material, or physical support for terrorist organizations (Neumann, 2017; Public Safety Canada, 2018; UNESCO, 2017).

Following 9/11, Western democracies began distinguishing extremism from violent extremism, reshaping counterterrorism strategies (Berger, 2018; Neumann, 2017). This shift enabled targeted interventions against those planning or engaging in violence, while acknowledging ideological roots. The rise of global religiously motivated violent ideologies accelerated policy development, bridging theory and practice—however, this period also saw harmful securitization (*see* Chap. 1).

2.3.4 Terrorism

Terrorism is a theoretically complex and politically contested phenomenon consisting of psychological, behavioral, and sociopolitical dimensions, and its conceptualization has evolved significantly overtime. Schuurman (2020, p. 14) defined the term *terrorism* as a form of "communication through extreme violence," describing it as a "purposefully bloody theatre" in which the primary goal is not murder itself, but rather spectacles of extremist violence used to draw attention to a cause, group, or grievance. This definition emphasizes the strategic, emotional, and communicative character of terrorism, positioning extreme violence as the tool or tactic for visibility and for advancing ideological goals with the intentional use of fear and chaos. From a legal perspective, many countries have adopted nation-specific definitions of terrorism, incorporating counterterrorism legislation into national security laws and anti-terrorism coordination between law enforcement services, intelligence agencies, and the military (Lynch et al., 2015; Neumann, 2017). However, because the legal definitions of terrorism remain contentious, with a universally agreed definition being absent and significant ongoing debate about what constitutes a terrorist act and who qualifies as a terrorist, global counterterrorism is challenged in different political and legal contexts (Lynch et al., 2015; Nacos, 2016). Many definitions emphasize the use of extremist violence against noncombatants to achieve political, religious, or ideological objectives (Lynch et al., 2015; Nacos, 2016). However, some definitions overlook the broader social, psychological, or political contexts where terrorism occurs, or concentrate on the violence itself rather than the varied ideological motivations (Neumann, 2017). This discrepancy complicates efforts to define terrorism or extremist violence, as the latter includes behaviors like radicalization, propaganda dissemination, and recruitment, beyond just terrorist actions.

2.4 Digital Media Environments and Online Radicalization

Understanding radicalization and the broader lexicon of countering violent extremism is more than an exercise in semantics. It shapes how we conceptualize threats, respond in case management and clinical practice, design future policy interventions, and ultimately, safeguard local or international communities. Yet, as radicalization unfolds within the boundless and dynamic domain of digital media environments, some traditional definitions and certain theoretical framings have been modified. This is because the introduction of the Internet has not simply provided new capabilities for those sympathetic to extremist aims or narratives, but transformed the conditions under which individuals are exposed to extremist aims and narratives, or can experience, grasp, and express sympathy for them. During the last quarter century, researchers generally focused on how technological functions are harnessed to advance specific goals or actions (Benigni et al., 2017; Gill et al., 2015, 2017; Whine, 1999).

Digital media technologies play a significant role in contemporary radicalization and extremist violence, influencing both the dissemination of extremist narratives and the ways individuals engage with ideological communities. It is widely accepted that Internet technologies and social media platforms act as powerful forces that can complement offline indoctrination events. However, an important question remains: can certain digital media environments or devices alone be sufficient for radicalization, or do individuals require their online experiences to be reinforced by interpersonal (or offline) relationships? Can the radicalization process unfold entirely in isolation, without face-to-face interactions with ideologically aligned individuals?

These questions challenge traditional conceptions of radicalization, which have long emphasized the role of interpersonal and social networks in fostering ideological commitment. As a result, terms such as "self-radicalization" have emerged to differentiate between individuals who engage with extremist communities through direct, offline interactions, and those who undergo similar processes independently, asynchronously forming relationships with online extremist milieus (Borum, 2011a).

However, the degree to which digital media technologies are considered important and influential to radicalization, particularly in the absence of any relevant offline social relationships, is a topic of debate. For instance, scholars contended that digital media environments can facilitate existing interest in extremist ideology or amplify existing conditions that encourage individuals to become more systematically exposed to extreme content and relationships online (Berger, 2018; Conway, 2012; Gill et al., 2015; Harris-Hogan & Barrelle, 2020; Koehler, 2014; Meleagrou-Hitchens et al., 2017; Powell et al., 2018). However, others argued that technologies, such as social media platforms like Meta and X, play an ideologically, psychologically, and behaviorally active role in affecting someone's experience in cases where existing interests or conditions are absent, which, in turn, compels us to rethink the criteria by which vulnerability is defined in the age of networked platforms (Edwards & Gribbon, 2013; Hutchinson & Droogan, 2022; Lovink, 2019; Sahani, 2018; Scrivens & Amarasingam, 2020; Zuboff, 2019).

Despite the degrees of potential influence, exposure to extremist content and online communities is considered a significant concern among already primed individuals—that is, those who possess predisposing psychological, social, or ideological vulnerabilities that make them particularly receptive to extremist narratives. This may include individuals who have experienced social isolation, marginalization, identity crises, or past exposure to extremist ideologies, making their interpretation and internalization of online content more likely to reinforce or accelerate their trajectory toward radicalization (McCauley & Moskalenko, 2017). For instance, websites like *Stormfront*[7] became more than a form of online communication, but a community-building tool and second home for those who reverberated white supremacy ideology and behavior (Bowman-Grieve, 2009; Scrivens, 2017). Extremists online, like every other person, had progressively integrated digital media technologies into their lives to satisfy urges for connection and community (Bowman-Grieve, 2009; Hale, 2012; Savci & Aysan, 2016). Unlike one-way forms of traditional media like newspapers, digital media technologies allow politically extreme communities or subcultures to freely exchange ideas, knowledge, and grievances (Langman, 2005; Perry & Scrivens, 2016). Subsequently, those who affectionately attach themselves to their virtual communities increase their personal sense of connectedness to the in-group and "solidarity across the world" (Perry & Scrivens, 2016, p. 17). Social workers must recognize the profound roles these virtual communities play in fulfilling unmet psychosocial conditions and consider strategies that provide healthier, pro-social alternatives to counter the appeal of extremist networks. Ecomapping (*discussed in* Chap. 3), can be a useful tool to kick-start dialogue with clients around different existing and absent communities, including in the online space, and their weaknesses or strengths.

The character and distribution of online violent extremist communities has changed considerably in previous decades. There are currently many different digital media environments hosting many different online violent extremist ideologies and discourses (Baele et al., 2020; Davey et al., 2020; Hutchinson et al., 2025). Mainstream social media platforms such as Meta and alternative platforms like Telegram have become prominent environments where hateful, violent, and extreme subcultural content and discussions continue to be consumed and communicated. While some alternative platforms had improved content moderation policies and operational regulations concerning extremist content, this has aided online migrations to even lesser regulated alternative platforms including 4chan and Gab (Amarasingam et al., 2021; Kingdon, 2020). Telegram, for example, is particularly favorable for its encrypted design, which allows extremist communities to communicate and organize with minimal risk of intervention, censorship, or content moderation (Ebner, 2020; Khouri & Kassire, 2016).

Furthermore, digital media technologies have effectively translated the exercise of othering into cyberspace, involving the portrayal of out-group members as

[7] Stormfront is a long-standing white supremacist webpage that hosts ideologically extreme conversations and is a prominent online location for extremist narratives and collective identities (Scrivens, 2017).

fundamentally different and inferior using digital media content or communications. Subsequently, *online othering* allows online extreme subcultural communities to engage in severe acts of discrimination and violence at a distance, without facing immediate, or any, social, physical, or legal consequences for their actions. For instance, the Government of the United Kingdom (2020) stated, "even if they may not be illegal in all circumstances," the Internet "can be used to harass, bully or intimidate, especially people in vulnerable groups or in public life" with "serious psychological and emotional impact." Alternative platforms have historically provided an online environment where controversial public figures or influencers who are banned from mainstream platforms can migrate to in order to continue to repurpose current events to mobilize extreme ideological interests, revitalizing solidarity and anxieties against the Other (Baele et al., 2020; Hutchinson, 2019).

It is important to note that digital media platforms, especially social media, are far from benign, passive tools or indulgences, but are profoundly influential ecosystems shaping each person's psychological and interpersonal development (Lovink, 2019; Zuboff, 2019). For instance, the impact of recommendation algorithms and algorithmic ranking has gained considerable academic attention in recent years (Whittaker, 2024). The manipulative power of personalization algorithms has important implications for how social workers assess a person's relationship to these platforms and adjoining technologies like smart phones (Hutchinson et al., 2025; Hutchinson & Droogan, 2022). Research suggested that personalization algorithms are neither psychologically nor socially neutral but are intentionally crafted to maximize user engagement by effectively learning about and tailoring persons' digital media digests, to further acquiesce and steer their attention and behaviors toward user engagement and consumer purchases (Zuboff, 2019). A recent study on the algorithmic recommendations of YouTube Shorts and TikTok found that algorithms are increasingly promoting extremist, toxic content (e.g., male supremacism and anti-feminist content) more so than neutral or positive content (Baker et al., 2024). The trust users place in certain mainstream platforms and machine-learning recommendations can also suggest that social media platforms have the potential to significantly alter political and ideological viewpoints, progressively more extreme in nature or controversial or characterized by outrage and polarization (Howard et al., 2018; Reis et al., 2015; Ribeiro et al., 2019; Suresh et al., 2020).

Despite considerable evidence demonstrating the influence of digital media technologies, some scholars remain skeptical about the emphasis placed on their role in radicalization. This skepticism is primarily rooted in a baseline issue: while many individuals are exposed to hateful or extremist content online, only a small fraction undergo radicalization, and even fewer commit acts of violence. Additionally, these critiques highlight that radicalization is a multifaceted process—one that accumulates experiences and shapes personal identity in ways that cannot be reduced to time spent in digital media environments, especially given the importance of broader sociopolitical contexts and social, offline interactions (Gill et al., 2015; Sahani, 2018). In clinical practice, social workers should exercise caution when interpreting the role of digital media in radicalization, recognizing that each client's relationship to digital technology is unique. Perhaps, a client who spends the majority of their time online in extremist spaces or is exposed to extremist content, with limited offline engagement, may be at greater risk of radicalization than someone who engages with these online communities but has strong offline mitigating factors such as stable employment and supportive, pro-social relationships. Therefore, it is essential to view digital media as one component within a broader, contextually grounded understanding of an individual's path to radicalization (Burke, 2011; Hussain & Saltman, 2014; Kenney, 2010).

To conclude this section, digital media technologies generally function as a dynamic facilitator, and sometimes accelerator or medium, of radicalization processes and violent extremism. However, the influence of technologies like social media operate within a constellation of mechanisms that shape individuals' beliefs, behaviors, and ideological affiliations. Social media platforms serve as decisive nodes in a broader networked process, connecting individuals to ideological networks, reinforcing extremist worldviews through algorithmically driven online spaces, and amplifying online extremist content with unprecedented speed and reach. The personalized nature of content delivery, coupled with the often-unregulated alternative platforms and the role of online influencers in digital recruitment strategies, intensifies users' emotional resonance with extremist material, complicating efforts to disrupt radicalization pathways online. However, such digital media technologies do not operate in a vacuum. They interact with offline experiences, existing grievances, and socioemotional dynamics outside of cyberspace, serving as accelerants or enablers. For social workers to develop more effective frameworks and CVE strategies, these complexities ought to be understood through an ecological, multi-disciplinary lens, integrating online and offline interventions.

2.5 Conclusion: Implications for Social Work and Online Interventions

This chapter has outlined the CVE field's theoretical and terminological diversity and its implications in different operational contexts, aiming to illustrate that terminologies are neither theoretically nor practically static; they are shaped by various cultural, organizational, and disciplinary influences. It remains important to acknowledge that counterterrorism theory and terminology used in CVE largely originated from a post-9/11, over-securitized framing, which can create tension with social work's core values. Social work prioritizes empowerment, human dignity, and social justice (among other values) which may subsequently be at odds with approaches driven by security concerns or narrow risk thinking. As discussed in Chap. 1, this tension will require social workers to critically engage with CVE frameworks, ensuring that interventions are not only evidence-based but also aligned with social work's commitment to fostering trust, dignity, and autonomy in vulnerable populations.

One of the key takeaways from this chapter is the importance of adopting a nuanced, multidimensional framework when dealing with radicalization. A holistic understanding, based on systemic, non-linear, and person-in-environment approaches, is essential for social workers engaged in CVE interventions. By embracing this complexity, social workers can identify the immediate and more obvious signs of radicalization, but also the more subtle social, psychological, systemic, and practical details that contribute to radicalization pathways. This chapter therefore supports Bouhana's (2019) suggestion that radicalization and extremism are ecological outcomes emerging from systemic interactions between an individual's various personal, environmental, and cognitive factors to influence their individualized trajectory into ideologically extreme positions.

As discussed, radicalization pathways are influenced in dialogue with online and virtual communities and impacted by digital algorithmic features, artificial intelligence, and technological advancements as well as by the spread and pervasiveness of mainstreamed racism and hate across virtual milieus. CVE intervention programs have begun to explore outreach approaches and psychosocial support services within the online space. For instance, developed by Moonshot, the so-called Redirect Method is a digital media technology that uses targeted advertising to send individuals who searched for violent extremist content alternative pro-social and pro-democratic messaging (Yuzva Clement et al., 2022). Furthermore, and more recently, Moonshot has partnered with several CVE intervention programs, including in Canada, the United States, and New Zealand, to facilitate online outreach and off-ramping. When an at-risk online user searches for violent extremist content, they are presented with an advertisement and offer to connect virtually with a CVE professional (e.g., via chat, text messaging, email, phone calls), or with a locally anchored community-based CVE intervention program, highlighting the importance of integrated online–offline care and digitized services (Moonshot, 2023). This emerging online-to-offline targeted outreach approach, such as on Google Search and YouTube, was designed in collaboration with CVE intervention programs and is grounded in psychosocial, voluntary, and confidentiality principles (Moonshot, 2023). By referring to Reamer (2017), Gheorghe and Yuzva Clement (2023) cautioned that practitioners aiming to engage in such virtual spaces require advanced skills in digital professionalism, online and hybrid service delivery, and client and personal safety. CVE practitioners need to prioritize their own safety across digital, physical, organizational, and mental–emotional domains. Exposure to traumatic content online can lead to vicarious trauma and burnout, while risks such as doxxing and online harassment underscore the need for strong digital safeguards (e.g., VPNs, secure devices, and careful management of one's online footprint). Physical and organizational safety can be strengthened by using work-specific accounts, selecting safe and appropriate meeting locations, developing clear safety and security protocols, and avoiding the disclosure of personal information. Mental health can be supported through team-based approaches, regular breaks, supervision, and intentional self-care practices. Overall, it is essential for practitioners to be familiar with—and consistently engage in—these safety measures.

Within the realm of our digitalized world, scholars have also pointed to the value of critical thinking and digital literacy as tools for empowerment against online hate and extremism in the first place. Recommendations, which can be used in psycho-education, include digital inclusion paired with digital literacy, emotional intelligence, and critical thinking competences, while rejecting risk-averse approaches that downplay the social benefits of Internet and social media use for young people (Caton & Landman, 2022). Similarly, Kurglova (2023) found that critical education on detecting QAnon-related disinformation on social media paired with strong family ties can be an effective way to address online radicalization and disinformation risk. Online gaming and adjacent communities can also be spaces for online victimization and exposure to hate and extremism (Hartgers & Leidig, 2023; RAN, 2022). Therefore, young people, as will be discussed in Chap. 4, need to be educated about the risks of cyber-victimization both within and outside of gaming platforms given that boundaries between online gaming, social networks, and associated platforms are blurred (Du et al., 2021).

References

Alberda, D. L., Duits, N., van den Bos, K., Autsema, A., & Kempes, M. (2022). Identifying risk factors for Jihadist terrorist offenders committing homicide: An explorative analysis using the European Database of Terrorist offenders. *Frontiers in Psychology, 13*, 1000186. https://doi.org/10.3389/fpsyg.2022.1000186

Amarasingam, A., Maher, S., & Winter, C. (2021). *How telegram disruption impacts Jihadist platform migration*. Centre for Research and Evidence on Security Threats. CREST Creative Commons.

Angove, J. (2024). Stochastic terrorism: Critical reflections on an emerging concept. *Critical Studies on Terrorism, 17*(1), 21–43. https://doi.org/10.1080/17539153.2024.2305742

Argentino, M.-A., Barrett, G., & Tyler, M. B. (2024). *764: The intersection of terrorism, violent extremism, and child sexual exploitation*. Global Network on Extremism & Technology. Retrieved July 9, 2025, from https://gnet-research.org/2024/01/19/764-the-intersection-of-terrorism-violent-extremism-and-child-sexual-exploitation/

Awan, A. N., Hoskins, A., & O'Loughlin, B. (2012). *Radicalisation and media: Connectitivity and terrorism in the new media ecology*. Routledge.

Baele, S. J., Brace, L., & Coan, T. G. (2020). Uncovering the far-right online ecosystem: An analytical framework and research agenda. *Studies in Conflict & Terrorism*, 1–21. https://doi.org/10.1080/1057610X.2020.1862895

Baker, C., Ging, D., & Andreasen, M. B. (2024). *Recommending toxicity: The role of algorithmic recommender functions on YouTube shorts and TikTok in promoting male supremacist influencers*. DCU Anti-Bullying Centre. Retrieved March 11, 2025, from https://antibullyingcentre.ie/publication/recommending-toxicity-the-role-of-algorithmic-recommender-functions-on-youtube-shorts-and-tiktok-in-promoting-male-supremacist-influencers/

Bakker, E. (2006). *Jihadi terrorists in Europe: Their characteristics and the circumstances in which they joined the jihad; an exploratory study*. Clingendael.

Baram, L. (2019). *They are not us: A philosophical exploration of violent extremism*. University of Sydney.

Benigni, M. C., Joseph, K., & Carley, K. M. (2017). Online extremism and the communities that sustain it: Detecting the ISIS supporting community on Twitter. *PLoS One, 12*(12). https://doi.org/10.1371/journal.pone.0181405

Berger, J. M. (2018). *New research report: The alt-right Twitter census*. VOX –Pol.

Biene, J., & Junk, J. (2017). Salafismus und Dschihadismus. Konzepte, Erkenntnisse und Praxisrelevanz der Radikalisierungsforschung. In J. Kärgel (Ed.), *"Sie haben keinen Plan B". Radikalisierung, Ausreise, Rückkehr—zwischen Prävention und Intervention* (pp. 115–128). Bundeszentrale für politische Bildung.

Borum, R. (2011a). Radicalization into violent extremism I: A review of social science theories. *Journal of Strategic Security, 4*(4). https://doi.org/10.5038/1944-0472.4.4.1

Borum, R. (2011b). Radicalization into violent extremism II: A review of conceptual models and empirical research. *Journal of Strategic Security, 4*(4). https://doi.org/10.5038/1944-0472.4.4.2

Bouhana, N. (2019). *The moral ecology of extremism: A systemic perspective* (United Kingdom Commission for Countering Extremism). University College London: Department of Security and Crime Science. Retrieved March 11, 2025, from https://assets.publishing.service.gov.uk/media/5d8b7993ed915d036da0e677/Bouhana-The-moral-ecology-of-extremism.pdf.

Bowman-Grieve, L. (2009). Exploring "Stormfront": A virtual Community of the Radical Right. *Studies in Conflict & Terrorism, 32*(11), 989–1007. https://doi.org/10.1080/10576100903259951

Brown, A. (2017). What is hate speech? Part 1: The myth of hate. *Law and Philosophy, 36*(4), 419–468. https://doi.org/10.1007/s10982-017-9297-1

Burke, J. (2011, December 16). Al-Shabab's tweets won't boost its cause. The Guardian. http://www.theguardian.com/commentisfree/2011/dec/16/al-shabab-tweets-terrorism-twitter.

Cable, S., Walsh, E. J., & Warland, R. H. (1988). Differential paths to political activism: Comparisons of four mobilization processes after the three Mile Island accident. *Social Forces, 66*(4), 951–969. https://doi.org/10.1093/sf/66.4.951

Carthy, S. L., & Schuurman, B. (2024). Adverse childhood experiences, education, and involvement in terrorist violence: Examining mediation and moderation. *Journal of School Psychology, 106*, 101348. https://doi.org/10.1016/j.jsp.2024.101348

Caton, S., & Landman, R. (2022). Internet safety, online radicalisation and young people with learning disabilities. *British Journal of Learning Disabilities, 50*(1), 88–97. https://doi.org/10.1111/bld.12372

Centre for the Prevention of Radicalization Leading to Violence. (2024). *The radicalization process*. CPRLV. Retrieved March 11, 2025, from https://info-radical.org/en/the-radicalization-process/.

Chan, V., & Derenne, J. (2021). *Transition-age youth mental health care. Bridging the gap between pediatric and adult psychiatric care*. Springer.

Conway, M. (2012). From al-Zarqawi to al-Awlaki: The emergence and development of an online radical milieu. *CTX: Combating Terrorism Exchange, 2*(4) Article 4.

Corner, E., Gill, P., & Mason, O. (2016). Mental health disorders and the terrorist: A research note probing selection effects and disorder prevalence. *Studies in Conflict & Terrorism, 39*(6), 560–568. https://doi.org/10.1080/1057610X.2015.1120099

Corner, E., Taylor, H., & Bragias, A. (2023). Modelling drivers of grievance-fuelled violence. *Australian Institute of Criminology*. https://doi.org/10.52922/ti78924

Corner, E., Taylor, H., Vegt, I. V. D., Salman, N., Rottweiler, B., Hetzel, F., Clemmow, C., Schulten, N., & Gill, P. (2021). Reviewing the links between violent extremism and personality, personality disorders, and psychopathy. *The Journal of Forensic Psychiatry & Psychology, 32*(3), 378–407. https://doi.org/10.1080/14789949.2021.1884736

Cottee, S. (2021). Incel (E)motives: Resentment, shame and revenge. *Studies in Conflict & Terrorism, 44*(2), 93–114. https://doi.org/10.1080/1057610X.2020.1822589

CPN-PREV. (2025). *Commonalities and differences in risk factors for extremist violence and related forms of violence: An umbrella review.* Canadian Practitioners Network for the Prevention of Extremist Violence.

Crossett, C., & Spitaletta, J. (2010). *Radicalization: Relevant psychological and sociological concepts [Prepared for the U.S. Army Asymmetric Warfare Group]*. The Johns Hopkins University Applied Physics Laboratory. Retrieved March 11, 2025, from https://info.publicintelligence.net/USArmy-RadicalizationConcepts.pdf

Davey, J., & Ebner, J. (2017). *The fringe insurgency—connectivity, convergence and mainstreaming of the extreme right.* Institute for Strategic Dialogue. Retrieved March 11, 2025, from https://www.isdglobal.org/isd-publications/the-fringe-insurgency-connectivity-convergence-and-mainstreaming-of-the-extreme-right/.

Davey, J., Hart, M., & Guerin, C. (2020). *An online environmental scan of right-wing extremism in Canada* (Interim Report). Institute for Strategic Dialogue. Retrieved March 11, 2025, from https://www.isdglobal.org/wp-content/uploads/2020/06/An-Online-Environmental-Scan-of-Right-wing-Extremism-in-Canada-ISD.pdf.

Dawson, L. (2022). Olivier Roy and the "Islamization of Radicalism": Overview and critique of a theory of Western Jihadist radicalization. *Journal for Deradicalization, 30*, 81–116. https://journals.sfu.ca/jd/index.php/jd/article/view/575/335.

Dawson, L. (2019). Clarifying the explanatory context for developing theories of radicalization: Five basic considerations. *Journal for Deradicalization, 18*, 146–184. https://journals.sfu.ca/jd/index.php/jd/article/view/191/145.

Deloughery, K., King, R. D., Asal, V., & Forest, J. (2012). Close cousins or distant relatives? The relationship between terrorism and hate crime. *Crime and Delinquency, 58*(5), 663–688. https://doi.org/10.1177/0011128712452956

Droogan, J., & Hutchinson, J. (2024). Right-wing extremism in Australia. In R. Gunaratna & K. Petho-Kiss (Eds.), *A research agenda for far-right violence and extremism* (pp. 181–210). Edward Elgar Publishing.

Du, Y., Grace, T. D., Jagannath, K., & Salen-Tekinbas, K. (2021). Connected play in virtual worlds: Communication and control mechanisms in virtual worlds for children and adolescents. *Multimodal Technologies and Interaction, 5*(5), 27. https://doi.org/10.3390/mti5050027

Ebner, J. (2020). *Going dark: The secret social lives of extremists*. Bloomsbury Publishing.

Edwards, C., & Gribbon, L. (2013). Pathways to violent extremism in the digital era. *The RUSI Journal, 158*(5), 40–47. https://doi.org/10.1080/03071847.2013.847714

Gartenstein-Ross, D., & Blackman, M. (2019). Fluidity of the fringes: Prior extremist involvement as a radicalization pathway. *Studies in Conflict & Terrorism*, 1–24. https://doi.org/10.1080/1057610X.2018.1531545

Gartenstein-Ross, D., Goodman, J. D., & Grossman, L. (2009). *Terrorism in the West 2008: A guide to terrorism events and landmark cases*. FDD Press.

Gartenstein-Ross, D., & Plant, T. (2023, September 20). *An evolving threat landscape: Composite violent extremism and prevention efforts*. GNET. Retrieved March 11, 2025, from https://gnet-research.org/2023/09/20/an-evolving-threat-landscape-composite-violent-extremism-and-prevention-efforts/.

Gentry, C. E. (2022). Misogynistic terrorism: It has always been here. *Critical Studies on Terrorism, 15*(1), 209–224. https://doi.org/10.1080/17539153.2022.2031131

Gheorghe, R. M., & Yuzva Clement, D. (2023). Weaponized autism: Making sense of violent internalized ableism in online Incel communities. *Deviant Behavior*, 1–15. https://doi.org/10.1080/01639625.2023.2268253

Gill, P., Corner, E., Conway, M., Thornton, A., Bloom, M., & Horgan, J. (2017). Terrorist use of the internet by the numbers. *Criminology & Public Policy, 16*(1), 99–117. https://doi.org/10.1111/1745-9133.12249

Gill, P., Corner, E., Thornton, A., & Conway, M. (2015). *What are the roles of the internet in terrorism? Measuring online behaviours of convicted UK terrorists*. VOX –Pol.

Government of the United Kingdom. (2020, December 15). *Online harms white paper*. Government of the United Kingdom. Retrieved March 11, 2025, from https://www.gov.uk/government/consultations/online-harms-white-paper/online-harms-white-paper.

Hale, W. C. (2012). Extremism on the World Wide Web: A research review. *Criminal Justice Studies, 25*(4), 343–356. https://doi.org/10.1080/1478601X.2012.704723

Hafez, M., & Mullins, C. (2015). The radicalization puzzle: A theoretical synthesis of empirical approaches to homegrown extremism. *Studies in Conflict and Terrorism, 38*(11), 958–975. https://doi.org/10.1080/1057610X.2015.1051375

Harris-Hogan, S., & Barrelle, K. (2020). Young blood: Understanding the emergence of a new cohort of Australian Jihadists. *Terrorism and Political Violence, 32*(7), 1391–1412. https://doi.org/10.1080/09546553.2018.1473858

Hartgers, M., & Leidig, E. (2023). *Fighting extremism in gaming platforms: A set of design principles to develop comprehensive P/CVE strategies*. International Centre for Counter-Terrorism—ICCT. Retrieved March 11, 2025, from https://www.icct.nl/publication/fighting-extremism-gaming-platforms-set-design-principles-develop-comprehensive-pcve.

Hegghammer, T. (2006). Terrorist recruitment and radicalization in Saudi Arabia. *Middle East Policy, 13*(4), 39–60. https://doi.org/10.1111/j.1475-4967.2006.00269.x

Hirschfield, A. F., Christmann, K., Wilcox, A., Rogerson, M. C., & Sharratt, K. (2012). *Process evaluation of preventing violent extremism programmes for young people*. Retrieved March 11, 2025, from https://www.semanticscholar.org/paper/Process-Evaluation-of-Preventing-Violent-Extremism-Hirschfield-Christmann/93d7278d4f9ffb31ff36d9f06a733e9114d2520e.

Horgan, J. (2008). From profiles to pathways and roots to routes: Perspectives from psychology on radicalization into terrorism. *The Annals of the American Academy of Political and Social Science, 618*(1), 80–94. https://doi.org/10.1177/0002716208317539

Horgan, J. (2009). *Walking away from terrorism: accounts of disengagement from radical and extremist movements*. Routledge.

Horgan, J. (2014). *The psychology of terrorism* (2nd ed.). Routledge.

Horgan, J. (2019, October 26). *RESOLVE 2019 global forum: John Horgan on the the psychology of terrorism* [video recording]. YouTube. https://www.youtube.com/watch?v=xDWomrw2O84.

Howard, P., Kollanyi, B., Bradshaw, S., & Neudert, L.-M. (2018). *Social Media, News and Political Information during the US Election: Was polarizing content concentrated in swing states?* Retrieved July 9, 2025, from https://demtech.oii.ox.ac.uk/wp-content/uploads/sites/12/2017/09/Polarizing-Content-and-Swing-States.pdf.

Hussain, G., & Saltman, E. M. (2014). *Jihad trending: A comprehensive analysis of online extremism and how to counter it*. Quilliam. Retrieved March 11, 2025, from https://www.quilliaminternational.com/shop/e-publications/jihad-trending-a-comprehensive-analysis-of-online-extremism-and-how-to-counter-it-2/.

Hutchinson, J. (2019). The new-far-right movement in Australia. *Terrorism and Political Violence*, 1–23. https://doi.org/10.1080/09546553.2019.1629909

Hutchinson, J. (2023). From flowers to far-right extremists: A genealogy of ecology in terrorism and extremism studies. *Critical Studies on Terrorism*, 1–25. https://doi.org/10.1080/17539153.2023.2218156

Hutchinson, J. (2024). Right-wing extremist threat landscape in Canada: Avenues for coalescence and Transnationalization. In R. Gunaratna & K. Petho-Kiss (Eds.), *A research agenda for far-right violence and extremism* (pp. 45–74). Edward Elgar Publishing.

Hutchinson, J., Bell, K., & Ganesh, B. (2025). 'You think that you'd get laid if it wasn't for advancements in technology'?: A sociological analysis of marginalised masculinity in involuntary celibate communities. In S. Lakhani & A. Amarasingam (Eds.), *The sociology of violent extremism* (pp. 149–178). Oxford University Press.

Hutchinson, J., & Droogan, J. (2022). Far-right 'Reactions': A comparison of Australian and Canadian far-right extremist groups on Facebook. *Behavioral Sciences of Terrorism and Political Aggression*, 1–28. https://doi.org/10.1080/19434472.2022.2112742

Jackson, S. (2019). *A schema of right-wing extremism in the United States*. International Centre for Counter-Terrorism (ICCT). Retrieved March 11, 2025, from https://www.icct.nl/publication/schema-right-wing-extremism-united-states.

Kelly, C. R., & Aunspach, C. (2020). Incels, compulsory sexuality, and fascist masculinity. *Feminist Formations, 32*(3), 145–172. https://doi.org/10.1353/ff.2020.0044

Kenney, M. (2010). Beyond the Internet: Mētis, Techne, and the Limitations of Online Artifacts for Islamist Terrorists. *Terrorism and Political Violence, 22*(2), 177–197. https://doi.org/10.1080/09546550903554760.

Kessler, D. (2016). *Capture: Unraveling the mystery of mental suffering* (Reprint edition). Harper Wave.

Khalil, J., Horgan, J., & Zeuthen, M. (2020). The ABC model: Clarifications and elaborations. *Terrorism and Political Violence, 34*(3), 460–467. https://doi.org/10.1080/09546553.2020.1776703

Khalil, J., Horgan, J., & Zeuthen, M. (2019). The attitudes-behaviors corrective (ABC) model of violent extremism. *Terrorism and Political Violence, 34*(3), 425–450. https://doi.org/10.1080/09546553.2019.1699793

Khouri, L., & Kassire, A. (2016). *Tech for Jihad: Dissecting Jihadists' digital toolbox*. Flashpoint. Retrieved March 11, 2025, from https://a51.nl/sites/default/files/pdf/TechForJihad.pdf.

King, M., & Taylor, D. M. (2011). The radicalization of homegrown jihadists: A review of theoretical models and social psychological evidence. *Terrorism and Political Violence, 23*(4), 602–622. https://doi.org/10.1080/09546553.2011.587064

Kingdon, A. (2020). *The gift of the gab: The utilisation of COVID-19 for neo-Nazi recruitment*. Global Network on Extremism & Technology. Retrieved March 11, 2025, from https://gnet-research.org/2020/05/07/the-gift-of-the-gab-the-utilisation-of-covid-19-for-neo-nazi-recruitment/.

Koehler, D. (2014). The radical online: Individual radicalization processes and the role of the internet. *Journal for Deradicalization, 1*, 116–134. https://journals.sfu.ca/jd/index.php/jd/article/view/8/8.

Kruglova, A. (2023) *Understanding conspiracist radicalisation: QAnon's mobilisation to violence*. ICCT. Retrieved March 11, 2025, from https://www.icct.nl/publication/understanding-conspiracist-radicalisation-qanons-mobilisation-violence.

Langman, L. (2005). From virtual public spheres to global justice: A critical theory of internetworked social movements. *Sociological Theory, 23*(1), 42–74. https://doi.org/10.1111/j.0735-2751.2005.00242.x

Lovink, G. (2019). *Algorithmic hate: Brenton Tarrant and the dark social web by Luke Munn*. Institute of Network Cultures. Retrieved March 11, 2025, from http://networkcultures.org/blog/2019/03/19/luke-munn-algorithmic-hate-brenton-tarrant-and-the-dark-social-web/.

Lösel, F., King, S., Bender, D., & Jugl, I. (2018). Protective factors against extremism and violent radicalization: A systematic review of research. *International Journal of Developmental Science, 12*(1–2), 89–102. https://doi.org/10.3233/DEV-170241

Lygre, R. B., Eid, J., Larsson, G., & Ranstorp, M. (2011). Terrorism as a process: A critical review of Moghaddam's "Staircase to Terrorism". *Scandinavian Journal of Psychology, 52*(6), 609–616. https://doi.org/10.1111/j.1467-9450.2011.00918.x

Lynch, A., McGarrity, N., & Williams, G. (2015). *Inside Australia's anti-terrorism Laws and Trials*. NewSouth.

MacKinnon, N., & Colman, I. (2016). Factors associated with suicidal thought and help-seeking behaviour in transition-aged youth versus adults. *Canadian Journal of Psychiatry. Revue Canadienne de Psychiatrie, 61*(12), 789–796. https://doi.org/10.1177/0706743716667417

McCauley, C., & Moskalenko, S. (2008). Mechanisms of political radicalization: Pathways toward terrorism. *Terrorism and Political Violence, 20*(3), 415–433. https://doi.org/10.1080/09546550802073367

McCauley, C., & Moskalenko, S. (2017). Understanding political radicalization: The two-pyramids model. *American Psychologist, 72*(3), 205–216. https://doi.org/10.1037/amp0000062

McCauley, C. (2020). The ABC model: Commentary from the perspective of the two pyramids model of radicalization. *Terrorism and Political Violence, 34*(3), 451–459. https://doi.org/10.1080/09546553.2020.1763964

McCormick, G. H. (2003). Terrorist decision making. *Annual Review of Political Science, 6*(1), 473–507. https://doi.org/10.1146/annurev.polisci.6.121901.085601

McKenzie, A., & O'Brien, D. (2024). The evolution of estimated time of arrival: The city of Toronto's CVE program. *Journal for Deradicalization, 39*, 94–128. https://journals.sfu.ca/jd/index.php/jd/article/view/911.

Meleagrou-Hitchens, A., Alexander, A., & Kaderbhai, N. (2017). The impact of digital communications technology on radicalization and recruitment. *International Affairs, 93*(5), 1233–1249. https://doi.org/10.1093/ia/iix103

Mills, C. E., Freilich, J. D., & Chermak, S. M. (2015). Extreme hatred: Revisiting the hate crime and terrorism relationship to determine whether they are "Close Cousins" or "Distant Relatives". *Crime & Delinquency, 63*(10), 1191–1223. https://doi.org/10.1177/0011128715620626

Moghadam, P. A. (2006). In F. P. E. in the D. of P. S. L. Weinberg & B. Eubank (Eds.), *The roots of terrorism*. Chelsea House Publications.

Moghaddam, F. M. (2005). The staircase to terrorism: A psychological exploration. *The American Psychologist, 60*(2), 161–169. https://doi.org/10.1037/0003-066X.60.2.161

Moonshot. (2023). *Countering radicalization to violence in Ontario and Quebec. Canada's first online-offline interventions model.* Retrieved March 11, 2025, from https://149736141.v2.pressablecdn.com/wp-content/uploads/Moonshot_Countering-Radicalization-to-Violence-in-Ontario-and-Quebec-1.pdf.

Nacos, B. L. (2016). *Terrorism and counterterrorism* (5th ed.). Routledge.

Nash, S. (2021). *Terrorism and the terrorized: How the "Terrorism" label is informed and applied to a violent attack in Canada. Research Brief.* Canadian Network for Research on Terrorism, Security and Society.

Neumann, P. (2017). *Countering violent extremism and radicalisation that Lead to terrorism: Ideas, recommendations, and good practices from the OSCE region.* Organization for Security and co-operation in Europe. Retrieved March 11, 2025, from https://www.osce.org/chairmanship/346841.

Neumann, P. R. (2013). Options and strategies for countering online radicalization in the United States. *Studies in Conflict & Terrorism, 36*(6), 431–459. https://doi.org/10.1080/1057610X.2013.784568

Neyroud, P., Aziz, A., & Kubicek, B. (2024). Update on Campbell's countering violent extremism programme. *Campbell Systematic Reviews, 20*(2), e1387. https://doi.org/10.1002/cl2.1387

Odag, Ö., Leiser, A., & Boehnke, K. (2019). Reviewing the role of the Internet in radicalization processes. *Journal for Deradicalization, 21*. https://journals.sfu.ca/jd/index.php/jd/article/view/289

O'Donnell, C., & Shor, E. (2022). "This is a political movement, friend": Why "incels" support violence. *The British Journal of Sociology, 73*(2), 336–351. https://doi.org/10.1111/1468-4446.12923

Organization for the Prevention of Violence. (2022, September 2). *'Salad-bar' extremism on the rise in Canada, report says. 'Salad-Bar' Extremism on the Rise in Canada*. Retrieved July 9, 2025, from https://preventviolence.ca/salad-bar-extremism-on-the-rise-in-canada-report-says/.

Paniagua, F. A. (2005). Some thoughts on the 'Staircase to Terrorism'. *American Psychologist, 60*(9), 1038–1039. https://doi.org/10.1037/0003-066X.60.9.1038b

Perry, B., & Scrivens, R. (2016). White pride worldwide: Constructing global identities online. In J. Schweppe & M. Austin Walters (Eds.), *The globalization of hate: Internationalizing hate crime?* (pp. 65–78). Oxford University Press. https://doi.org/10.1093/acprof:oso/9780198785668.003.0005

Powell, A., Stratton, G., & Cameron, R. (2018). *Digital criminology: Crime and justice in digital society*. Routledge.

Public Safety Canada. (2018). *National Strategy on countering radicalization to violence*. Canada Centre for Community Engagement and Prevention of Violence (Government of Canada). Retrieved March 11, 2025, from https://www.publicsafety.gc.ca/cnt/rsrcs/pblctns/ntnl-strtg-cntrng-rdclztn-vlnc/ntnl-strtg-cntrng-rdclztn-vlnc-en.pdf.

Purdue, S. (2022). *Ideological nihilism and aesthetic violence. Mass shooters and online antisocial subcultures.* Global Network on Extremism & Technology. Retrieved July 9, 2025, from https://gnet-research.org/2022/07/13/ideological-nihilism-and-aesthetic-violence-mass-shooters-and-online-antisocial-subcultures/.

RAN. (2022). *Integrating the online dimension into offline pedagogical practices.* RAN Conclusion Paper. Retrieved March 11, 2025, from https://home-affairs.ec.europa.eu/system/files/2022-06/ran_y-e_integrating_online_dimension_into_offline_pedagogical_practices_8-9032022_en.pdf.

Ravndal, J. A., & Bjørgo, T. (2018). Investigating terrorism from the extreme right: A review of past and present research. *Perspectives on Terrorism, 12*(6), 5–22. https://pt.icct.nl/article/investigating-terrorism-extreme-right-review-past-and-present-research

RCMP. (2024). *Five-eyes insights—young people and violent extremism: A call for collective action.* Royal Canadian Mounted Police. Retrieved March 11, 2025, from https://rcmp.ca/

en/corporate-information/publications-and-manuals/five-eyes-insights-young-people-and-violent-extremism-call-collective-action.

Reamer, F. G. (2017). Evolving ethical standards in the digital age. *Australian Social Work, 70*(2), 148–159. https://doi.org/10.1080/0312407X.2016.1146314

Reis, J., Benevenuto, F., Vaz de Melo, P. O. S., Prates, R., Kwak, H., & An, J. (2015). Breaking the news: First impressions matter on online news. In Proceedings of the 9th International Conference on Web and Social Media (ICWSM 2015) (pp. 357–366). AAAI Press. https://doi.org/10.1609/icwsm.v9i1.14619

Ribeiro, M. H., Ottoni, R., West, R., Almeida, V. A. F., & Meira, W. (2019). Auditing radicalization pathways on YouTube. arXiv:1908.08313 [cs.CY]. https://doi.org/10.48550/arXiv.1908.08313

Rousseau, C., Frounfelker, R., Ngov, C., & Crocker, A. (2022). Clinical services addressing violent extremism: The Quebec model. *International Journal of Forensic Mental Health, 22*(3), 222–232. https://doi.org/10.1080/14999013.2022.2147254

Rousseau, C., Miconi, D., Frounfelker, R. L., Hassan, G., & Oulhote, Y. (2020). A repeated cross-sectional study of sympathy for violent radicalization in Canadian college students. *The American Journal of Orthopsychiatry, 90*(4), 406–418. https://doi.org/10.1037/ort0000444

Roy, O. (2013). *Holy ignorance: When religion and culture part ways.* Translated by Ros Schwartz. London.

Sageman, M. (2008). *Leaderless Jihad: Terror networks in the twenty-first century*. University of Pennsylvania Press.

Sahani, S. (2018). *Examining the association between social media and violent extremism: A social learning approach.* University of Maryland, College Park. Retrieved March 11, 2025, from http://search.proquest.com/docview/2278079013/abstract/A4F3A67983DE40A9PQ/1.

Sarma, K. M., Carthy, S. L., & Cox, K. M. (2022). Mental disorder, psychological problems and terrorist behaviour: A systematic review and meta-analysis. *Campbell Systematic Reviews, 18*, e1268. https://doi.org/10.1002/cl2.1268

Savci, M., & Aysan, F. (2016). Relationship between impulsivity, social media usage and loneliness. *Educational Process: The International Journal, 5*(2), 106–115. https://doi.org/10.12973/edupij.2016.52.2

Schuurman, B. (2020). Research on terrorism, 2007–2016: A review of data, methods, and authorship. *Terrorism and Political Violence, 32*(5), 1011–1026. https://doi.org/10.1080/09546553.2018.1439023

Schuurman, B., & Taylor, M. (2018). Reconsidering radicalization: Fanaticism and the link between ideas and violence. *Perspectives on Terrorism, 12*(1), 3–22. https://www.jstor.org/stable/26343743?seq=1

Schuurman, B., Lindekilde, L., Malthaner, S., O'Connor, F., Gill, P., & Bouhana, N. (2018). End of the lone wolf: The typology that should not have been. *Studies in Conflict & Terrorism, 42*(8), 771–778. https://doi.org/10.1080/1057610X.2017.1419554

Scrivens, R. (2020). Exploring radical right-wing posting behaviors online. *Deviant Behavior*, 1–15. https://doi.org/10.1080/01639625.2020.1756391

Scrivens, R., & Amarasingam, A. (2020). Haters Gonna "Like": Exploring Canadian far-right extremism on Facebook. In M. Litter & B. Lee (Eds.), *Digital extremisms: Readings in violence, radicalisation and extremism in the online space: Vol. Palgrave studies in cybercrime and cybersecurity* (pp. 63–89). Springer Nature.

Scrivens, R. M. (2017). *Understanding the collective identity of the radical right online: A mixed-methods approach* [Thesis, Arts & Social Sciences: School of Criminology]. http://summit.sfu.ca/item/17632.

Silber, M., & Bhatt, A. (2007). *Radicalization in the West: The homegrown threat.* New York Police Department NYPD Intelligence Division. Retrieved March 11, 2025, from https://info.publicintelligence.net/NYPDradicalization.pdf.

Silber, M. D. (2012). *The Al Qaeda factor: Plots against the West.* University of Pennsylvania Press.

Silva, D. M. D. (2018). 'Radicalisation: The journey of a concept', revisited. *Race & Class, 59*(4), 34–53. https://doi.org/10.1177/0306396817750778

Sizoo, B., Strijbos, D., & Glas, G. (2022). Grievance-fueled violence can be better understood using an enactive approach. *Frontiers in Psychology, 13.* https://doi.org/10.3389/fpsyg.2022.997121

Stunden, C., Zasada, J., VanHeerwaarden, N., Hollenberg, E., Abi-Jaoudé, A., Chaim, G., Cleverley, K., Henderson, J., Johnson, A., Levinson, A., Lo, B., Robb, J., Shi, J., Voineskos, A., & Wiljer, D. (2020). Help-seeking behaviors of transition-aged youth for mental health concerns: Qualitative study. *Journal of Medical Internet Research, 22*(10), e18514. https://doi.org/10.2196/18514

Suresh, H., Lao, N., & Liccardi, I. (2020, July 9). Misplaced trust: Measuring the interference of machine learning in human decision-making. *AI—history and trust*. 12th ACM Web ScienceConference2020. https://www.youtube.com/watch?v=rxQeZPwCgvU&feature=youtu.be.

Tinnes, J. (2023). Individual and contextual factors of radicalisation. *Perspectives on Terrorism, 17*(4), 210–271. https://pt.icct.nl/sites/default/files/2023-12/RS%201.pdf

Tran, H. (2025). *How male grievance fuels radicalisation and extremist violence*. ASPI. Retrieved July 25, 2025, from https://www.aspistrategist.org.au/how-male-grievance-fuels-radicalisation-and-extremist-violence/.

UNESCO. (2017). *Youth led guide on prevention of violent extremism through education*. UNESCO Digital Library. Retrieved March 11, 2025, from https://unesdoc.unesco.org/ark:/48223/pf0000260547.

Veldhuis, T., & Staun, J. (2009). *Islamist radicalisation: A root cause model*. Netherlands Institute of International Relations Clingendael.

Vergani, M., & Hutchinson, J. (2024). Ecosystems of hate: Understanding the relationship between terrorism, hate crime, and hate speech. In J. Hawdon & M. Costello (Eds.), *Research handbook on hate and hate crimes in society* (pp. 301–319). Edward Elgar Publishing. https://doi.org/10.4337/9781803925738.00025

Vermeulen, F., & Visser, K. (2021). *Preventing violent extremism in The Netherlands: Overview of its broad approach* (128). Revista CIDOB d'Afers Internacionals. Retrieved March 11, 2025, from https://www.cidob.org/en/articulos/revista_cidob_d_afers_internacionals/128/preventing_violent_extremism_in_the_netherlands_overview_of_its_broad_approach.

Vidino, L., & Hughes, S. (2015). ISIS in America: From Retweens to Raqqa. In *Program on extremism* (pp. 1–31). The George Washington University. Retrieved March 11, 2025, from https://extremism.gwu.edu/sites/g/files/zaxdzs2191/f/downloads/ISIS%20in%20America%20-%20Full%20Report.pdf

Whine, M. (1999). Cyberspace-A new medium for communication, command, and control by extremists. *Studies in Conflict & Terrorism, 22*(3), 231–245. https://doi.org/10.1080/105761099265748

Whittaker, J. (2024). *Predicting harm among incels (involuntary celibates): The roles of mental health, ideological belief and social networking (accessible) [Independent Report]*. United Kingdom Government's Commission for Countering Extremism. Retrieved March 11, 2025, from https://www.gov.uk/government/publications/predicting-harm-among-incels-involuntary-celibates/predicting-harm-among-incels-involuntary-celibates-the-roles-of-mental-health-ideological-belief-and-social-networking-accessible.

Wilson, C. (2020). Nostalgia, entitlement and victimhood: The synergy of white genocide and misogyny. *Terrorism and Political Violence*, 1–16. https://doi.org/10.1080/09546553.2020.1839428

Wolfowicz, M., Weisburd, D., & Hasisi, B. (2021). Examining the interactive effects of the filter bubble and the echo chamber on radicalization. *Journal of Experimental Criminology., 19*, 119–141. https://doi.org/10.1007/s11292-021-09471-0

Yuzva Clement, D. (2022). Post-migrant dynamics of Islam: Muslim youth and Salafism in Germany. In S. Zarrabi-Zadeh, T. K. Gugler, & A. Omerika (Eds.), *Dynamics of Islam in the modern world* (pp. 141–174). Brill. https://doi.org/10.1163/9789004512535_008

Yuzva Clement, D., Kiefer, J., Hassan, G., & King, M. (2022). Countering radicalization to violence in Canada. A multi-sector perspective. In R. Ceylan & M. Kiefer (Eds.), *Der islamische Fundamentalismus im 21. Jahrhundert. Analyse extremistischer Gruppen in westlichen Gesellschaften* (pp. 325–345). Springer VS.

Zuboff, S. (2019). *The age of surveillance capitalism: The fight for a human future at the new frontier of power*. Ingram Publishers.

Chapter 3
Disengagement and Exiting from Violent Extremism: Assessment, Case Management, and Clinical Practice

3.1 Introduction

In the field of countering violent extremism (CVE), there is a growing recognition of the value that social work theory and practice bring to the design, implementation, and evaluation of disengagement, diversion, and exit interventions for individuals at risk of or engaged in violent radicalization. This chapter delves into key theories and intervention modalities, including case management and clinical approaches, and discusses the complexities inherent in assessment and intervention processes. By employing common theories and approaches such as trauma-informed practice and the bio-psycho-social-spiritual model, this chapter lays the groundwork for understanding how disengagement from violent extremism can be achieved within multi-sectoral and social work-led contexts. Emerging evidence from secondary and tertiary CVE programs underscores the necessity of embedding CVE more firmly within the domain of social work. As argued by several scholars and discussed throughout this book, clinical or psychosocial CVE is increasingly being recognized as a promising and new field within social work practice. This chapter explores the intricacies of interventions and case management in the context of disengagement from radicalization to violence, beginning with the definitional challenges surrounding key concepts such as deradicalization and disengagement. The lack of consensus on these terms and their implications for direct intervention practice are critically examined. The chapter then introduces case management as a structured, client-centered approach designed to guide individuals away from extremist attitudes and behaviors through tailored interventions. These interventions often necessitate coordination across multiple systems, including mental health, education, and sometimes law enforcement. By drawing on social work's bio-psycho-social-spiritual model, effective direct practice and case management emphasize the importance of holistic engagement and assessment. Assessment and intervention tools are crucial for understanding and addressing the multiple vulnerabilities, needs, and strengths of

D. Yuzva Clement et al., *Social Work and Countering Violent Extremism*, SpringerBriefs in Social Work, https://doi.org/10.1007/978-3-032-07086-9_3

individuals, thereby developing interventions that not only mitigate risk but also empower individuals within their environments, promoting sustainable disengagement from extremism. This chapter highlights the need for specialized competencies among social workers and other psychosocial professionals, for example in trauma-informed care. It also emphasizes the importance of evaluating and adapting interventions to meet the evolving needs of clients, advocating for a strengths-based approach to support clients' social reintegration.[1] By equipping readers with practical concepts and theoretical frameworks, this chapter aims to provide a comprehensive understanding of how social work can effectively contribute to CVE efforts, fostering a safer and more inclusive society.

3.2 Definitional Challenges

As with the concept of radicalization, there is still no consensus on the definition of *de*radicalization and related terms (Baaken et al., 2021). Both in research and in practice, there is a lively ongoing debate about the appropriate terminology used to describe an individual's departure from violent extremist affiliations, actions, and beliefs. Depending on the professional, institutional, organizational, or even geographic context, there are numerous terms in circulation to describe the process of distancing away from violent extremist attitudes and behaviors. As an umbrella term, CVE can be broken down into different sub-concepts or logics and, as the following sections will highlight, the concepts in question carry different meanings and implications for how practice is conceptualized and implemented.

Koehler (2016) referred to *deradicalization* as the notion of individual or collective attitudinal change and the re-pluralization of political concepts and values, fostered or guided by an external party or individual commitment. By referring to Barrelle (2015), Koehler argued "that successful disengagement or deradicalization involves both the exit from the extremist milieu and the re-engagement of the non-extremist environment" (2016, p. 80). To this two-fold process, he added the idea of re-pluralization as a third layer to underscore the psychological mechanism of individual distancing on the one hand, and the development of value diversity or complexity in thinking on the other. According to Koehler, "effective deradicalization intervention therefore must be hand-tailored to the individual radicalization process and psychological driving factors behind the commitment" (2016, p. 81).

Scholars often distinguish between *cognitive deradicalization* (i.e., turning away from extremist attitudes and beliefs) and *habitual/behavioral disengagement* (i.e., abandoning extremist actions and behaviors, a process that can also be described as

[1] In this chapter, we use the term *reintegration* with the caveat that it assumes a prior state of integration—an assumption that may not hold for individuals from marginalized or excluded communities or who experience severe social isolation and loneliness. For some, integration was never fully realized, making "reintegration" a potentially misleading term (Walkenhorst et al., 2020).

behavioral distancing; Altier et al., 2014; Bjørgo & Horgan, 2008; Feddes, 2015; Horgan & Braddock, 2010). Ceylan and Kiefer (2018) considered the concept *behavioral distancing* to be a more realistic alternative to deradicalization, as they doubted the possibility of complete cognitive deradicalization or value-based re-pluralization. To these authors, behavioral distancing involves a fundamental change away from certain *actions* and *behaviors*, especially from violence to non-violence: "it takes place without changing the cognitive aspects, i.e. it is a distancing at the action level, which makes it possible to remain [within] the extremist patterns of thought" (Baaken et al., 2021, p. 5). Similarly, the concept of *disengagement* focuses on the dissociation from extremist, terrorist, and violent activities and behaviors (Irwin, 2015). This is also in line with other scholars who understand disengagement as distancing oneself from violence and leaving extremist groups, movements, or organizations without necessarily abandoning extremist ideological views (Dechesne, 2011; Rabasa et al., 2010). For Barrelle (2015), disengagement involves social identity–change processes related to group membership, the development of an individualized sense of self, and the search for alternative persons, groups, or entities to identify with. Earlier, Paternoster and Bushway (2009) similarly emphasized internal self-concept transformation as a core mechanism in the move away from harmful or violent behavior. Paternoster and Bushway argued that desistance occurred when individuals rejected a "feared self" and moved toward an attainable, prosocial "possible self." A cognitive or emotional trigger then initiates a reevaluation of one's identity and future trajectory. Here, desistance was understood primarily as an identity-based transformation rather than a response to external pressures. However, research has also found that deradicalization and disengagement is not a prerequisite for the other, suggesting that, while there often seems to be correlation, there is no proof for causality between both processes (Morrison et al., 2021). Furthermore, these processes are not without significant challenges. In fact, research has identified a range of difficulties—including those related to mental health—that can arise during disengagement pathways, describing these experiences as forms of "post-exit distress" (Meredith & Horgan, 2024), which may persist long after individuals have left extremist movements.

Considering deradicalization includes work unfolding at the pre-criminal or non-criminal space, such a concept is thought to infringe upon the guaranteed rights of freedoms of persons, groups, and communities. For instance, as observed in iterations of certain government-led CVE initiatives, deradicalization and associated racialized stereotypes contributed to the heightened criminalization, securitization, and surveillance of certain groups, especially Muslim communities (Awan, 2012; Thomas, 2018; *see* Chap. 1).

3.2.1 Prevention and the Public Health Model

On top of the apparent diversity of concepts discussed above, there is the parallel use of the prevention paradigm and classification models, deriving from public health and medical sectors (Ceylan & Kiefer, 2018). The two prominent prevention models are Caplan's distinction between *primary, secondary,* and *tertiary prevention*, and Gordon's differentiation between *universal*, *selective*, and *indicated prevention* (Ceylan & Kiefer, 2018; El-Mafaalani et al., 2016). Both models interpret CVE, or deradicalization and disengagement, taking place toward one end of the spectrum, by equating it to either secondary to tertiary or selective to indicated prevention.

In general terms, primary (or universal) prevention is directed at the general population, or subsets of the population, to ensure the development of problems is thwarted. This is typically achieved through public education, community or population empowerment, and skill-building in a range or areas. Secondary (or selective) prevention is focused on problems at an early stage. It aims to prevent further problem development through targeted efforts during an opportunity window where there is relative ease to address and change problematic development. Lastly, tertiary (or indicated) prevention focuses on addressing a problem development (such as violent extremism) at a serious or manifest stage aimed at countering it from worsening or causing additional damage (Sheafor & Horejsi, 2006; Sjøen, 2020; Hassan et al., 2021a, 2021b).

Nonetheless, some scholars have been far more critical and cautioned against the adoption, or called for partial adaptations, of public health approaches for the sake of CVE, arguing that the proximity of CVE to securitization and national security will lead to "losing the trust of communities characterized that way" (Eisenman et al., 2020, p. 58). These authors called for a critical integration of public health with an emphasis on interdisciplinary scientific development in support of evidence-based programs paired with rigorous program evaluation (Eisenman et al., 2020).

It is further argued to embed CVE efforts into existing community-based programs and services and to expand local capacity and resources. From a conceptual perspective, then, community-based programs and social services can integrate preventing violent extremism (PVE) segments into their existing approaches and adapt their services, making their programming, as put by Eisenman and colleagues, *PVE-relevant,* while those program types specially addressing cases of violent radicalization, particularly in the tertiary prevention realm, are described by the authors as *PVE-specific* (Eisenman et al., 2020).

Oftentimes, CVE initiatives or programs tend to focus on identifying and mitigating different kinds of deficits or social risks, typically conceptualized as risk factors associated with radicalization pathways, such as social isolation, economic disadvantage, and exposure to extremist ideologies (Heath-Kelly, 2017). However, as discussed in Chap. 2, there are no root causes or *static* risk factors associated with violent radicalization. Risk is context-dependent and dynamic, and may arise when protective mechanisms are lacking.

Rather than static risk factors, Hassan and colleagues (2022a, 2022b) remind us that the assessment of *dynamic* risk factors, needs and vulnerabilities should be prioritized given that radicalization trajectories are non-linear processes. According to these authors, dynamic risk factors are aspects of a person or their social environment that, when modified, can result in changes in engagement/entrenchment in violent radicalization pathways (Hassan et al., 2022b). Sub-groupings of dynamic risk factors are, firstly, *stable risk factors* that tend to endure for a longer period of time (months, years) and require significant efforts to be modified. Secondly, there are *acute risk factors* which can signal the timing of heightened risk states within weeks, days, or even hours and might not be related to long-term risk; they are temporary disruptions or triggers in the psychological state or social environment of the individual (Hassan et al., 2022b).

And while the identification of risk factors and risk accumulation is undoubtedly important, a sole focus on deficits can overshadow the strengths and resilience within individuals, families, and communities. Social work, with its strengths-based perspective, traditionally emphasizes the capacities and resources that individuals and communities possess to overcome challenges. However, in the context of CVE, social work may be tasked to also integrate a more risk-centric approach, which could, if not paired with needs and strengths-based approaches, undermine its commitment to empowering clients and fostering resilience as well as promoting social justice (Cherney, 2018; Ragazzi, 2017; Stanley & Guru, 2015).

3.3 Secondary and Tertiary CVE: Emerging Evidence

The evidence base of secondary and tertiary CVE interventions is expanding; while it has produced recommendations, it has also pointed to gaps in the literature. As discussed above, secondary interventions or programs are directed to stop or slow the progression of certain deviant behavior, oftentimes taking place in pre-clinical settings (Eisenman et al., 2020). In the context of CVE, Hassan et al. (2021b) defined that secondary CVE interventions are directed toward populations that are identified as vulnerable to violent radicalization and extremism. One example of a secondary CVE intervention program is the integrated intervention model consisting of a psychoeducational support group and individual case management directed at youth that were perceived as being at-risk of joining the terrorist group Al-Shabaab in an East African urban city (Kolbe, 2019). Relevance in secondary prevention programs is placed on assessments with at-risk persons to detect and address behaviors before violence occurs (Eisenman et al., 2020); however, Hassan and colleagues showed that such assessment procedures are oftentimes not empirically validated (Hassan et al., 2021b). In a similar vein, Eisenman et al. (2020) discussed how threat assessments in school contexts might help inform risk assessment for violent radicalization, but that these threat assessments might miss cases where threat is not identified or imminent. Overall, secondary prevention programs serve clients believed to be at risk of engaging in violent extremism, assess and identify persons with social and mental health challenges, facilitate and navigate access to relevant services to address risk and adversities, and strengthen protective factors and community-based assets (Hassan et al., 2021b).

In their systematic evidence review of tertiary CVE programs, Hassan and colleagues found that such programs were targeted at various populations such as inmates, individuals under probation, arrested persons, members of extremist groups not under legal sanctions, youth work referrals, and members of online extremist groups (Hassan et al., 2021a), underscoring different methodological and organizational contexts as well as target group diversity (e.g., high-risk/intensity vs. low-risk/intensity, mandated vs. non-mandated clients, justice-involved vs. non-justice-involved). Hassan et al. (2021a) found that deradicalization programs were mainly focused on cognitive aspects of violent radicalization and ideology, like introspection, integrative complexity, pro-democratic values, critical thinking, and addressing and increasing one's sense of self/significance.

In contrast to deradicalization, disengagement efforts are predominantly focused on behavioral changes by assisting individuals in desisting from violent behavior, criminality, or the extremist group or milieu, without necessarily (or directly) addressing ideological components. As often seen in Canadian models, which also tend to work with clients across all forms of extremist ideologies including hybrid forms (Yuzva Clement et al., 2022), this is often achieved through case management and social reintegration programs which mainly focus on familial, peer mentorship, professional, educational, and societal integration including accessing and ensuring basic needs such as housing, health services, employment, as well as food security (Hassan et al., 2021a). Furthermore, tertiary CVE programs can also include complex psychosocial and clinical interventions such as counseling or treatment modalities that fall under psychotherapy (Hassan et al., 2021a). In community contexts, these multi-tiered services are considered wrap-around interventions that aim to immerse clients in programs and relationships of support.

Moreover, it is worth highlighting that different tertiary CVE programs (or their components) can lead to different outcomes. For example, psychosocial therapy-based programs can lead to healthy coping strategies and improved sense of mental health and trust, while social network-based programs can lead to increased engagement within interpersonal and intergroup contexts including improved positive engagement with prison staff, social workers, outreach workers, or family members (Hassan et al., 2021a). Concerning deradicalization, these authors concluded that "when deradicalization programs yielded positive results, it was often due to the social reintegration components of these programs" (Hassan et al., 2021a, p. 33), highlighting that it is more so the impact of social reintegration and psychosocial support services that further deradicalization, rather than directly addressing ideological components.

Despite ongoing efforts in research and evaluation, the evidence base regarding what works in preventing and countering violent extremism is weak, with a dearth of externally conducted program evaluations and few recent, but emerging, systematic evidence reviews and scientific studies (Brouillette-Alaire et al., 2025; Lösel et al., 2018; Hassan et al., 2021a, 2021b, 2022b; Wolfowicz et al., 2021). Recent research has repeatedly shown that interdisciplinary, multimodal, psychosocial, and multi-sectoral prevention efforts show positive effects in reducing risk and increasing resilience and protective factors against violent radicalization (Brouillette-Alaire et al., 2025; Hassan et al., 2021a, 2021b; Lösel et al., 2018). Further, a recent Delphi consensus building process concluded that paying attention to the social ecology of individuals who are at risk or involved in violent extremism are promising targets for secondary and tertiary CVE interventions to foster desistance and resilience (Hassan et al., 2022a).

With regard to social reintegration, Hassan et al. (2021a) and Brouillette-Alaire et al. (2025) concluded that social reintegration efforts seem more effective than deradicalization or religious counseling efforts, the latter often perceived as normative and potentially discriminatory for certain communities. Social reintegration programs assist individuals in returning to communities after incarceration or within community corrections contexts, but this approach also includes reintegrating individuals without a carceral history after their involvement with an extremist group, movement, or online milieu. In general, social reintegration emphasizes practical aspects and achieving positive change in several life domains such as education, housing, employment, accessing food, opening a bank account, accessing mental health services, finding structured leisure activities or community integration, and so on (Hassan et al., 2021a). Their research furthermore found that practitioners and program participants responded better to social reintegration interventions compared to deradicalization, with practitioners often observing that they lacked the adequate training or understanding to conduct deradicalization interventions (Hassan et al., 2021a). In sum, emerging research suggests that psychosocial CVE intervention programs, which focus on achieving positive outcomes in basic needs and life domains (i.e., social reintegration) and treating psychosocial vulnerabilities, can facilitate the disengagement from violent extremist thoughts and behaviors (Hassan et al., 2021a; King et al., 2025).

For example, in their 3-year longitudinal study, King et al. (2025) found that participation in a Canadian community-based and psychosocial CVE intervention program led to positive change in several life domains (including family relations, addictions, leisure activities, housing); participation directly reduced the clients' violent extremist thoughts and actions. In this study, a young client, who espoused white supremacist accelerationist ideology, was enrolled in the CVE intervention program for 36 months and experienced a reduction in their violent extremist thoughts and actions—not through active focus on the clients' ideology but rather through their psychosocial and social reintegration needs being met (King et al., 2025). The authors noted that although disengagement from violent extremism is a non-linear process, there can be several "setbacks during this period related to extremist beliefs, thoughts, and behaviours" (King et al., 2025, p. 14) and that building resilience to setbacks is key. Lastly, adjoining researchers recently showed how psychosocial CVE intervention programs increasingly draw on case management approaches to deliver this type of individually tailored work to clients within their social ecologies (Lewis et al., 2024; McKenzie & O'Brien, 2024).

Despite this variety in methodological and psychosocial intervention approaches, there seem to be six recurring approaches, methods, and associated objectives that are currently being applied within CVE intervention programs (Campelo et al., 2022; Hassan et al., 2021a; Stanley & Barracosa, 2024; Walkenhorst, 2022):

1. *Biographical/narrative approaches* aimed at working through and reflecting on the individual causes and drivers of radicalization pathways and supporting clients in goal setting for the future.

2. *Deradicalization*, which encourages reflection on extremist ideology and thought patterns and supports the development or re-pluralization of pro-democratic values.
3. *Social reintegration and multi-system navigation*, focused on supporting clients (oftentimes through case management) with regard to a variety of practical implications as well as basic and complex needs such as access to education, housing, employment, therapy, healthcare, food, and so forth, including strengthening personal and social skills.
4. *Individual therapy-based counseling or psychotherapy* aimed at psychosocial assessment, treatment, referrals, sometimes psychiatric stabilization, development of coping skills, mental health well-being, empowerment, and strengthening personal and social skills.
5. *Family-based, systemic counseling, and psychoeducation* aimed at supporting family members, caregivers, or other professionals, which may include group work, to develop emotional, reflection, and communication skills within one or more social system(s) (e.g., family, school, neighborhood) and to raise awareness and provide learning opportunities about radicalization pathways and digital literacy for instance; related are restorative justice approaches used in contexts of community conflict and tension.
6. *Political-historical democracy education and civic literacy,* referring to educational initiatives that aim to foster critical awareness of political systems, historical contexts, and democratic principles and values. This approach emphasizes that understanding the historical roots of social injustices, political ideologies, and systemic inequalities, while promoting active engagement in democratic processes is an important aspect in disengagement and upstream prevention. It equips individuals and communities with the tools and knowledge to critically analyze extremist narratives, resist divisive ideologies, and build resilience through democratic participation and leadership.

While some programs may specialize in one intervention approach or modality depending on their organizational mandate or practice setting, programs may also use a combination of these approaches relevant to each individual case or setting. Depending on the severity of the case, CVE intervention programs may apply a complex case management approach grounded in trauma-informed practice.

To the seasoned psychosocial professional and social work reader, these basic methods and associated goals of countering violent extremism practices listed above are closely related to those of different subfields of social work (e.g., direct clinical practice, family counseling, etc.). Some of these approaches are genuine methods developed within social work. However, few scholars have discussed this intersection and called for greater attention to the social work and CVE nexus. As discussed in Chap. 1, it is against the backdrop of social work involvement in CVE that some have argued that CVE should be classified as a new social work area of practice. We urge practitioners working in generalist social work practice to utilize their skills and competencies and to not engage in what Chivers (2018) described as bracketing off or service denial, which might add to the perceived disenfranchisement that clients adhering to extremism typically uphold.

Social work researchers might perceive CVE as a new field for social work investigation and knowledge development. Researchers that work closely with CVE practitioners consider the overemphasis on extremist ideology as a key driver for radicalization to be inappropriate (Hassan et al., 2021a; Weilnböck & Uhlmann, 2018). Similarly, discussions with practitioners seem to confirm this perspective regarding deradicalization and disengagement processes (Hassan et al., 2022a; Ohlenforst et al., 2022). These practitioners point out that in most cases other key issues are at stake, such as addressing individual needs, adversities, trauma, and long-term or acute personal crises (Figlestahler & Schau, 2020; Mücke, 2016). As such, we argue that social work can help demystify CVE in order to ground it in a variety of psychosocial assessments and professional intervention frameworks and approaches.

3.4 Social Work's Bio-Psycho-Social-Spiritual Model and Assessment

The bio-psycho-social-spiritual model holds great prominence both in social work theory and practice (Burns et al., 2018). It provides a holistic knowledge base for client engagement, assessment, intervention, and termination in social work (Burns et al., 2018). In generalist social work, practitioners should capture the person-in-environment—that is, the person themselves, the wider social, political, economical, and the spiritual, cultural dimensions that affect the client. There is no unified theory in social work and many theories and approaches, some of which will be discussed here, only address parts of human behavior. Hence, the bio-psycho-social-spiritual model aims to tie different facets together and provide a comprehensive understanding of a client's system (Heinonen & Spearman, 2001). Intersectionality theory adds that identities and experiences of discrimination cannot be explained within discrete boundaries. For instance, gender *or* race cannot be analyzed separately; they must be understood through their intersection, such as the combined experience of sexism *and* racism, thereby embracing the complexity of human behavior (Birdsey & Kustner, 2021). While good assessment is knowledge-guided, evidence-based, and client-centered, the social worker's theoretical frame of reference and lived experiences can also influence and give rise to biases within the assessment process. As such, social workers cannot do this type of work without first knowing themselves psychologically, culturally, and politically.

The bio-psycho-social-spiritual model supports practitioners to explore and assess different dimensions of the client and use varied knowledge bases for assessment and interventions. Typically, the knowledge bases include biological/biomedical, psychodynamic, cognitive-behavioral, family and socio-cultural as well as environmental, structural, critical, feminist, and Indigenous theories (Burns et al., 2018; Heinonen & Spearman, 2001). Overall, the bio-psycho-social-spiritual model unites our thinking in terms of both the *social* determinants of health and the *health* determinants of social well-being, underscoring that the issues that clients face are typically multidimensional and may require an interdisciplinary, multi-level assessment and inter-agency treatment approach (Burns et al., 2018). George Engel's earlier biopsychosocial model informed the development of the so-called 4 Ps model of case formulation (Bolton, 2014; Weerasekera, 2009), which will be discussed below. The 4 Ps model is widely used by mental health professionals and has become a common case formulation framework in social work practice (Bogo, 2018). The following paragraphs explore theories and knowledge bases within the bio-psycho-social-spiritual model and how it can support interventions to CVE.

With regard to biological theories, the field of neuroscience has made significant expansion to help better understand the biological underpinning of human behavior; however, biology and society do not exist in a vacuum and have a lasting and intersecting impact on individuals and their families (Burns et al., 2018). Abuse, neglect, and trauma intersect with biology, especially with regard to mental illness, since trauma impacts brain development and bodily reactions. Trauma-based theories explain how traumatized clients often re-enact their trauma or a trauma scenario with others including clinicians (Berzoff, 2011). Also, ongoing stress, such as from racism, systemic abuse, lack of access to housing, limited economic opportunities, and microaggressions can affect brain development, raise cortisol levels and blood pressure, increase tendency to infections, and cause hyperarousal and hypervigilance (van der Kolk, 2014). Together, the early environment, grinding everyday stress, and big and small trauma can imprint onto the brain, body, and mold the neural networks, establishing neuroanatomical and biochemical set points for emotions, memory, and attachment. Further, every client has genetic predispositions, for example, for diabetes or depression. Berzoff (2011) reminds us that some clients survive and even thrive in traumatogenic settings; others may be cushioned socioeconomically but are biologically predisposed to chronic mental illness or to the negative effects of trauma. Part of assessment is often to identify any current diagnoses or histories of diagnoses, mental and/or physical.

Psychological theories such as psychodynamic and cognitive-behavioral theories provide important aspects for clinical work:

> In every setting, and with every population, we try to understand how a person has developed psychologically; has taken in and metabolized the social world; has or has not experienced microaggressions based on disability, race, sexual orientation, culture, or language; and might have internalized social stigma. (Berzoff, 2011, p. 133)

Psychodynamic theories attend to understanding clients' unconscious motivation and how humans are psychologically shaped by early experiences (often those developed during childhood). Against this backdrop of complexity, it becomes apparent how clients "cannot just change with an injunction from us," meaning psychosocial practitioners (Berzoff, 2011 p. 136). Psychodynamic theories, operationalized through attachment-based therapy for instance, provide knowledge about the developmental needs of children and whether they have been met.[2] They also

[2] Criticism of psychodynamic theories include that they are conservative and often prescribed fixed and stereotypical roles. Intersectionality and critical race theory have influenced current writings in psychodynamic theory.

shed light on the clinical interaction between client and clinician and how transference and countertransference unfold.

For example, for Hartmann every person needs an *average and expectable (predictable) environment* in which the person can expect that the world will adapt to them and in which the person can adapt to the environment (Berzoff, 2011). Another somewhat different psychodynamic concept is what Winnicott described as the *holding environment*, referring to the creation of a safe, nonjudgmental environment that fosters the natural maturation and development of the true self and full potential of each child (Berzoff, 2011). Where there have been traumatic circumstances, such as violence or abuse and without mediating factors, such as supporting parents or caregivers, significant others, and supportive educational environments or community groups, "many clients will inexplicably seek out toxic relationships because those are the only kinds they have known" (Berzoff, 2011, p. 144). Ecosystems theories underscore that when persons cannot find a good niche or spaces where they can grow and prosper, social exchanges become predominantly negative and social, economic, and personal problems often emerge (Heinonen & Spearman, 2001). Cognitive-behavioral theories and treatments add further knowledge regarding psychological dimensions of human behavior.

Clients' social contexts are typically influenced by how power, social justice, and control unfolds within society. The social context shapes capabilities (or the lack of thereof) to form a holding environment, and social work pays great attention to structural forces such as poverty, injustice, and oppression and their impacts on clients, families, and communities. For example, in the United States, children growing up in poverty were offered medications four times as often as middle-class children receiving psychotherapy; in fact, poor children are frequently not seen for psychotherapy at all, resulting in serious side effects due to overmedication (Bezoff, 2011). When we work in inner cities, social workers and other professionals encounter a lack of habitable space and overcrowding; similarly, prisons are regularly described as places lacking adequate social services and support systems—especially for racialized communities. As discussed above, racism, trauma, and ongoing stress can cause physiological and psychological changes. Past trauma might result in, for example, fear, reactivity, hurtful self-representations, and hypersensitivity, which can exacerbate mental health problems such as depression, anxiety, or PTSD. A structural approach in social work examines how clients' problems are often caused by, or at least closely related to, failures in public and social institutions such as the economy, but also regarding access to safe housing, education, employment, transportation, social services, and healthcare. Here, a key task of practitioners is to advocate and support clients to gain control in their interactions with institutions and larger systems as well as to advocate for policy change in cases where social structures are harmful (Heinonen & Spearman, 2001). Today's cross-border rise of right-wing populist political parties or governments presents a profound challenge to the practice of social work, as populist movements are inherently illiberal, elevating the rights of powerful or dominant groups while eroding the rights of marginalized and scapegoated communities (Fischer & Dunn, 2019; Finn, 2021). For example, drawing on white supremacist ideologies and conspiracy narratives, populist governments have defunded social work programs serving 2SLGBTQIA+, BIPOC, and new immigrant communities (Reisch, 2019). Community organizing and counter-hegemonic advocacy networks play a critical role in ensuring that care, social justice, and belonging remain central to social work practice as a challenge to populist regimes as well as for mobilizing inter-sectoral resources and securing dispersed funding opportunities. Critical theory adds that racism, sexism, ableism, classism, ageism, and trans- and homophobia not only intersect in powerful and compelling ways and serve in the interest of the powerful to maintain the status quo, but also that these structural inequities manifest in clinical encounters (Burns et al., 2018). Critical theory reminds us that there are no unidimensional identities of people but that there are always multiple and intersecting identities; in other words, critical theory exhorts us to question essentialism.

With regard to spiritual dimensions and cultural values more broadly, social work has adopted the theory of cultural humility to grasp and appreciate another's experience. As put by Finn (2021, p. 60):

> Cultural humility requires social workers to acknowledge the partiality of their knowledge and open themselves to hearing and honoring another's story. [As such] one tries to apprehend meaning systems, values, ways of perceiving the world, and ways of constructing fundamental concepts such as personhood, family, wellness, and healing in ways that may be very different from one's own.

The bio-psycho-social-spiritual model not only posits that multiple dimensions of health and social well-being should be taken into consideration for holistic assessment and interventions, but also how these different dimensions are correlated. For clients at-risk of or engaged in violent radicalization, these knowledge bases offer multidimensional viewpoints to more holistically understand the interconnectedness of various risk factors and protective mechanisms. Assessing and interpreting these different dimensions and types of client data or information is a crucial part in social work in general and in specialized therapeutic settings in particular.

As a specialized field, CVE has seen a variety of *risk assessment tools* being developed over the past years. However, many of the risk assessment instruments for assessing violent extremism were not developed or intended for utilization within social work contexts. This situation provides challenges for social workers practicing in generalist roles, and social workers employed in psychosocial CVE intervention programs might also find it challenging to use risk assessment tools that are more narrowly security-focused than holistically client-centered. The bio-psycho-social-spiritual model reminds the social worker practicing in CVE to assess clients holistically and multidimensionally. The topic of risk assessment is an ongoing, lively discussion within the CVE community, and different agencies and organizations have found different ways of dealing with this matter. Could there be a way to support both public safety and client reintegration and rehabilitation, without the social worker compromising their ethical foundation? Heinonen and Spearman (2001, pp. 121–122) reflected on this intersection as follows:

> Particularly in fields like forensic psychiatry and corrections, a major responsibility of the social worker is to the public. The public, as represented by the judicial system, is really the primary client in a sense. The service that the social worker provides is usually to both protect the public at large and to help rehabilitate the offender.

3.4.1 Risk Assessment

Risk assessment describes a process that examines the probability of a certain event occurring (e.g., reengaging in criminal activity), the consequences of this event occurring, and how tolerable the consequences of the event occurring are (Lowrance, 1980).[3] In general, risk assessment is used in various fields including the insurance industry, the healthcare system, weather prediction, and the evaluation of the risk of violence posed by clients, patients, or inmates in correctional institutions. In the latter example, risk analyses are used as the basis for decisions regarding the setting of bail and conditions, the security classification and granting of parole hearings, as well as the assessment of the efficiency of measures (Pressman & Flockton, 2012).

Risk assessment for violent extremist ideological entrenchment or violent acting out is a relatively new area of application. The current state of research and practice regarding the assessment of risk of radicalization and violent extremism reveals a variety of challenges (Hassan et al., 2022b). For example, empirical research on risk factors and protective factors is not sufficiently developed to provide a solid foundation for what type of variables to include and not include in risk assessment tools. Another problem is that the presumed correlations between risk factors are sometimes not clear; related is the fact that pathways of violent radicalization can lead to multiple outcomes and the same *predictors* (risk factors) might not apply to the same outcome (Hassan et al., 2022b; *see* Chap. 2).

It is important to acknowledge that there can be fundamentally different operational logics of observing and understanding risk, depending on the institutional, professional background, and mandate of the observer. For example, due to the nature of their institutional mandate, security agencies tend to prioritize security risk toward society and broader national security (*society-centered risk assessment*) over individual client risk including client's corresponding needs, strengths, and rehabilitation (*client-centered risk and needs assessment*). In the context of violent extremism and terrorism, security authorities and law enforcement bear a significant degree of responsibility, supported by legal frameworks to prevent violence and ensure public safety. Considering the risk posed by individuals engaging in criminal and violent acts, such agencies are under significant pressure to act, particularly given the public scrutiny that often accompanies their decisions. As put by Hassan et al. (2022b, p. 1):

> While risk assessment in the security field is often used to guide surveillance, disruption, and/or sentencing, in the mental health and psychosocial field, it is mainly used to guide prevention and rehabilitative efforts. In the field of correctional psychology, rehabilitative approaches emphasize risk assessment's relevance for correctional intervention and service delivery or, in other words, risk reduction via treatment, capacity building, and social reinsertion.

To overcome current limitations in risk assessment tools for violent extremism, scholars have suggested to use structured professional judgment (SPJ) over actuarial

[3] The process of risk assessment can be either qualitative or quantitative. Frequently, such analyses are also associated with a general risk management plan, which outlines specific measures for addressing the risk, reducing the likelihood of its occurrence, and preventing its adverse effects.

scales to assess risk (Clemmow et al., 2025; Gill et al., 2023; Logan, 2021).[4] Furthermore, research has identified case formulation as a critical component of effective risk assessment, particularly in SPJ approaches. However, according to Clemmow et al. (2025) and Logan (2021), case formulation is missing in many commercially available CVE risk assessment instruments. Case formulation enables practitioners to move beyond static evaluations toward a dynamic, individualized understanding of the client, guiding scenario development, intervention planning, and monitoring change over time. In CVE contexts, this is especially valuable, and the 4 Ps model (Predisposing, Precipitating, Perpetuating, and Protective factors) is increasingly used to structure such formulations (Clemmow et al., 2025; Logan, 2023). This model has long been foundational in social work, highlighting the profession's deep expertise in contextual, person-centered analysis (Bogo, 2018). Given this alignment, there is a compelling case for greater involvement of social work in CVE, as its emphasis on contextualized, strengths-based formulation is well suited for the nuanced demands of prevention and intervention work for CVE. The following textbox presents two CVE-oriented tools that consist of structured professional judgment protocols.

Risk Assessment Tools for Violent Extremism: TRAP-18 and VERA-2R

TRAP-18 (Terrorist Radicalization Assessment Protocol) has been developed with the specific purpose of assessing the risk and/or recidivism of lone-actor terrorism, but has been retrospectively validated with other extremist populations (Clesle et al., 2024). TRAP-18 is primarily employed by law enforcement agencies, CVE organizations, forensic psychologists, and other mental health professionals to identify individuals who may engage or reoffend in targeted violence due to radicalization (Clesle et al., 2024). One of the key strengths of TRAP-18 is its structured professional judgment (SPJ) approach, which effectively integrates clinical judgment with a structured assessment framework. This approach allows for flexibility while still adhering to a standard protocol, rendering it particularly effective in identifying the distinctive behavioral patterns associated with lone-actor terrorists (Rousseau et al., 2024). The empirical basis of TRAP-18 is underscored by research conducted by Meloy and Gill (2016), which highlighted its utility in real-world scenarios and its capacity to avert potential lone-actor attacks. However, while TRAP-18 has several notable strengths, it also has certain inherent limitations. The tool's primary focus on lone-actor terrorism limits its applicability to broader contexts of violent extremism, such as those engaged in tiered group-based movements. Furthermore, despite its structured nature, critics have noted that while the SPJ model offers flexibility, it also poses challenges in maintaining consistency across different practitioners (Corner & Pyszora, 2022; Meloy & Roshdi, 2021).

[4] In general, structured professional judgment (SPJ) tools provide a framework for clinical judgment and practice; they specify which risk and protective factors should be assessed (Hassan et al., 2022b). As such, SPJ supports clinical focus and avoids focus on irrelevant factors or the omission of important factors. Factors included in SPJ must be empirically validated. Actuarial assessment tools aim to reliably determine the level of risk based upon statistical analysis leaving little room for professional input (Hassan et al., 2022b).

VERA-2R (Violent Extremism Risk Assessment, version 2 Revised) is a tool utilized to assess the risk of violent extremism in a comprehensive manner, encompassing both ideologically (i.e., non-religious) and religiously motivated violent extremism. Originally designed for assessment in prisons, VERA-2R is utilized by a diverse array of professionals, including law enforcement personnel, probation officers, and mental health practitioners, for the assessment of risk posed by individuals engaged in or vulnerable to extremist ideologies. It was developed in Canada and is now used widely in Europe and Australia for instance (Custodial Institutions Agency, n.d.). One of VERA-2R's advantages is its versatility, as it has been developed to be utilized in a multitude of scenarios pertaining to violent extremism, including group-based terrorism and religiously motivated violence. As Lloyd and Dean (2015) observed, the tool provides a comprehensive framework that guides practitioners through a systematic assessment of risk factors, thus offering a well-rounded approach to evaluating violent extremism. However, VERA-2R is not without its challenges either. Its broad scope and detailed nature can render the tool complex and time-consuming to apply (Duits & Kempes, 2023). Furthermore, the effective use of VERA-2R requires significant training and psychological expertise, which may limit its accessibility to certain organizations or professionals. Pressman and Flockton (2016) also observed that while the instrument is comprehensive, the requisite training and expertise can impede its broader adoption. Importantly, recent scholarship has found that VERA-2R lacks validation studies and therefore there is currently no predictive validity of VERA-2R as well as any other violent extremism risk assessment tool (CPN-PREV, 2025).

While both TRAP-18 and VERA-2R, and other such tools, rely on sound rationales, their level of empirical validation is currently weak (CPN-PREV, 2025; Hassan et al., 2022b; Scarcella et al., 2016). Another problem area is precision, bias, under- and overestimation, which is largely due to the low base rates of violent radicalization compared to other types of outcomes such as criminal recidivism, which could lead to stigmatization or false positives, and, in the context of underestimation, to premature releases within correctional contexts for instance.

What is sometimes missing in security-focused risk assessment is a focus on clients' strengths and needs, how relevant factors interact with another within the person, and how to move from assessment toward case planning and service delivery (Logan, 2023). As discussed earlier, case formulation plays a crucial role in bridging this gap because it offers a structured way to integrate risk with protective factors, personal history, and contextual dynamics. Due to the lack of validation studies of CVE risk assessment tools and in order to consider all relevant factors and information, research has also stressed the need to use CVE risk assessment tools in conjunction with other psychosocial assessment tools (CPN-PREV, 2025). Other authors have also highlighted the need for a comprehensive trauma-informed approach in CVE and counter-terrorism assessment (Marsden et al., 2024). Instead of viewing trauma as a decontextualized risk factor, risk assessment should frame trauma as a contextual factor for interpreting current and potential future trajectories (Marsden et al., 2024). According to these authors, many structured professional judgment tools for violent extremism identify risk factors for radicalization which can be understood as maladaptive responses to experiences of adversity and trauma (Marsden et al., 2024). In addition, using life-course thinking and socio-ecological theory contributes altogether to a more holistic understanding of radicalization pathways as an individual's attempt to adapt to adversity and trauma and meet unmet needs (Marsden et al., 2024). This perspective brings us closer to the need for psychosocial assessment in CVE interventions.

3.4.2 Psychosocial Assessment for CVE Interventions

Within CVE, there has been a growing demand for holistic needs- and resilience-based assessments as well as psychosocial assessments grounded within the bio-psycho-social-spiritual model (Rousseau et al., 2022; Ruf & Walkenhorst, 2021; Stanley & Barracosa, 2024; Wolf, 2019). For example, resilience assessment tools are essential for identifying protective factors and strengths within individuals and communities that can buffer against radicalization. Rather than solely upholding a deficit focus on risk, research by Ungar (2013) emphasized the importance of resilience in countering the impact of adverse conditions that might lead to radicalization, suggesting that these tools help practitioners identify key assets and strengths that can be leveraged in CVE interventions. For example, resilience theory has been used to inform the BRAVE Model (*Building Resilience Against Violent Extremism)* as well as the corresponding BRAVE scale[5] that measures resiliency factors and is used to inform case planning for program participants (Grossman et al., 2017; Grossman, 2021; Miramahdi, 2016). As seen with the bio-psycho-social-spiritual model and the aforementioned 4 Ps model, holistic assessments ensure that social workers and other professionals consider the full spectrum of an individual's circumstances, thus allowing for more comprehensive and tailored intervention planning and strategies. Another way to frame this approach is by using *socio-ecological* approaches. One example for such an approach is the social diagnostic toolkit GRIDD PRO, which was developed by the German nongovernmental CVE organization Violence Prevention Network (VPN). GRIDD PRO takes its inspiration from Western traditional social work spearheaded by Mary Richmond who published "*Social Diagnosis*" in 1917. Richmond's book discussed how the social surroundings influence the client's ability to cope and describes six sources of power for social casework available to clients: located in clients themselves, the family/household, the neighborhood, the wider social network, in civil service agencies, and in private and public organizations (Finn, 2021; Heinonen & Spearman, 2001). Richmond also introduced problem-solving as a key task within casework, comprising of problem identification, assessment, setting of goals and a contract or agreement for the work to be done, interventions, and finally ending or closing. Much of Richmond's work was later further developed and critiqued, and emphasis today is placed on client engagement and goal-setting frequently negotiated

[5] The following five risk and resilience domains are included in the BRAVE scale: cultural identity and connectedness, bridging capital, linking capital, violence-related behavior, and violence-related beliefs (Grossman et al., 2017). The authors noted that the scale needs further validation.

with clients (Heinonen & Spearman, 2001). Unlike medical or DSM-based diagnostics, social diagnostics should not be seen as a definitive or static categorization of an individual's condition. Instead of rigid and positivist[6] renditions of diagnostics, social diagnostics today might be best understood as a dynamic and ongoing process, grounded in social ecology thinking,[7] that requires continuous reassessment and revision of initial findings. The aim is not merely to label or classify, but also to generate hypotheses and contextualized understandings about the complex interplay of factors affecting an individual's well-being and social identify formation, which can then guide intervention strategies (Buttner et al., 2018).

Social Diagnostics in CVE: VPN's GRIDD PRO

Germany-based Violence Prevention Network (VPN) recently developed a comprehensive diagnostic toolkit specifically designed for frontline practitioners involved in disengagement, deradicalization, and rehabilitation efforts called GRIDD PRO—*Guiding Resilience, Integration, Disengagement & Development*. Based on the 3Rs methodology (risks, resources, and resonances), VPN's toolkit provides a structured approach to assessing the biographies, needs, emotional well-being, and social circumstances of individuals at risk or already engaged in extremist activities. The tool was developed in tandem with practitioners to design a toolkit suitable for everyday use. Drawing on insights from over 1800 cases of violent extremists and terrorist offenders and other at-risk individuals, the toolkit offers valuable lessons and best practices for professionals across sectors, including law enforcement, prisons and probation, health and social services, and civil society organizations. The social diagnostics approach provides practitioners with an overview of clients' resources, challenges, and development, supports practitioners in their decision-making concerning intervention, helps planning, and provides a structured documentation basis for monitoring and evaluation. By equipping practitioners with the necessary tools and framework, VPN's GRIDD PRO aims to facilitate effective case management and foster multidisciplinary collaboration, ultimately contributing to more successful outcomes in preventing and mitigating violent extremism.[8]

[6] Rigid and positivist renditions of diagnostics refer to diagnostic approaches that prioritize fixed categories, standardized criteria, and measurable outcomes, often rooted in a medical or scientific model; these approaches tend to overlook the complexity of social and cultural factors influencing individual experiences.

[7] A socio-ecological or multi-systems perspective recognizes that an individual's challenges or difficulties cannot be understood in isolation from the broader (socio-political) context of their lives. This perspective shifts the focus from solely treating the individual to also addressing the environmental and systemic changes needed to support the individual's well-being and promote resilience across multiple domains of their life.

[8] For more information, visit: https://www.vpn-academy.com/social-diagnostics/?lang=en.

Common to social work theory and practice and grounded within strengths-, ecology-, and needs-based approaches, Violence Prevention Network applies classic social diagnostic tools such as *ecomaps, genograms,* and *biographical lifelines* which are useful in mapping out relationships, adversity and conflict, socioeconomical circumstances, opportunities, and access to resources, and for identifying areas of vulnerability, gaps, strengths, and needs (Ruf & Walkenhorst, 2021; Sheafor & Horejsi, 2006). These instruments support social workers in developing a comprehensive view of clients or the family and contextualize them in their social environment, including available and absent resources and strengths, which is crucial for assessing and intervening in cases of violent radicalization. Usually, ecomaps or other such tools are utilized jointly by the client and social worker and help visualize the client's current (or even historical) social contexts, the quality of relationships, and relevant or absent support systems.

Evaluating an individual's subjective perspective of their social networks and support systems is a crucial component of network mapping, especially since a person's subjective contentment with their current relationships and support systems has a substantial impact on their health and well-being (Kupfer, 2018). Ecomapping can point the way for planning the process of disengagement that typically involves multiple actors within the network. As they also identify gaps, ecomaps point to potential growth and future connections to be made. They can also be used to evaluate interventions if they are applied consistently throughout the intervention process, as they provide a visual representation of changes over a given amount of time. It might be helpful to create retrospective maps that show various pivotal moments in people's life, such as before, during, or after radicalization, in order to better understand and document the client's life-course and needs. A similar tool is the *biographical lifeline approach*, through which practitioners and clients learn and understand how the quality or course of life has evolved over time and what factors (e.g., events, persons, groups, communities, institutions) have contributed both favorably and unfavorably to the client's life-course. Sheafor and Horejsi (2006, p. 261) remind us that ecomaps and other such tools do not objectively describe the client's network or support system, "but rather reflect the client's perceptions and beliefs. It is quite possible that a client may exaggerate or underestimate the importance of some people or simply forget to name others." Ultimately, these tools support engagement and reflection aimed at increasing client agency, but they also help translate assessment into case formulation and intervention planning. This is also more consistent with the most recent theories of radicalization, such as the Process Model (Horgan, 2014) and the Attitudes-Behavior Corrective Model (Khalil et al., 2019).

The integration of other psychosocial assessment tools, for instance regarding suicidality or other mental health challenges, are crucial in identifying underlying vulnerabilities that may predispose individuals to extremist ideologies, and signs of distress and mental health issues that could precipitate or perpetuate radicalization pathways (Marsden et al., 2024; Rousseau et al., 2022). For instance, this is especially important in cases of radicalization in some nihilistic violent extremist groups, which tend to specifically target youth demonstrating existing mental health challenges, suicidal ideation, low self-worth and feelings of hopelessness, and other forms of distress and maladaptive coping mechanisms. Given that these groups tend to encourage acts of self-harm and sometimes suicide, psychosocial assessment should capture self-harm and suicidal ideation screening. Such tools not only enhance the precision of assessment for risk and needs, but also support the case formulation of intervention plans that are responsive to the nuanced needs within the bio-psycho-social-spiritual continuum of those at risk of radicalization and related harms. Further, if clients present thoughts or behaviors that indicate mental illness or an undiagnosed mental condition, then a consideration could be to refer the client for psychiatric diagnosis. Ultimately, it is anticipated that holistic assessment could provide a functional equivalent to the risk assessment instruments utilized by law enforcement and other security professional groups, the latter being primarily focused on immediate public safety threats rather than long-term guidance to inform rehabilitative pathways.

As proposed by Heinonen and Spearman (2001) with regard to social workers practicing in forensic psychiatry, some CVE intervention programs have also found a way to integrate different assessments and logics, as the following example demonstrates. The Toronto-based CVE intervention program Estimated Time of Arrival (ETA), which is housed within a local mental health and social service provider called Yorktown Family Services, integrates various assessment tools to measure and address risks and needs across the social ecology of a client (McKenzie & O'Brien, 2024). The program uses the TRAP-18 to assess for risk of extremist violence every 3 months; ETA also uses the HEADS-ED model (Housing, Education/ Employment, Activities/Peers, Drugs, Suicidality, Emotions and Thought Disturbance, and Discharge) at intake and discharge, rating different areas of need and resources; the Suicide Assessment Kit (SAK) is also being used for adults with complex needs; and the Partners for Change Outcome Management Systems (PCOMS) is used to measure therapeutic outcomes (McKenzie & O'Brien, 2024). As McKenzie and O'Brien state, "this triangulation of collected and analyzed data supports ETA staff to clinically formulate intervention plans and goals that are responsive to all risk and needs that clients identify" (2024, p. 106). Clients are being discharged once threat to community is reduced, stability is reached in clients' abovementioned life domains, and once clients are part of a positive identity forming activity, such as education, employment, and/or volunteering; thereafter, discharged ETA clients are welcome to re-access services if need be (McKenzie & O'Brien, 2024). ETA also uses the Violent Threat Risk Assessment (VTRA) protocol in tandem with other community partners including law enforcement in situations where a client's risk of engaging in violence is significant. This includes joint risk management discussions with local partners as well as meetings with clients multiple times a week until their risk level is reduced (McKenzie & O'Brien, 2024). Indeed, at times significant assessment and community safety planning is needed for a short period of time, with the goal to prevent the need for an arrest and keeping the individual engaged in emerging pro-social activities and wrap-around supports. McKenzie and O'Brien's multidimensional and integrative assessment approach is supported by recent research that stressed not to use violent extremism assessment tools (such as VERA-2R or TRAP-18) as standalone tools, but in conjunction with other tools and as part of holistic risk and needs assessment frameworks and evidence-based clinical practice (CPN-PREV, 2025).

Lastly, recent research has stressed the need to add a trauma-informed perspective into violent extremism risk and needs assessment (Marsden et al., 2024). The authors underscored the need to better understand how individuals adapt to trauma when turning toward and away from violent extremism. In cases of violent extremism, research has shown that maladaptive trauma responses as well as cumulative effects of trauma can create contexts within which radicalization trajectories are more likely to occur (Marsden et al., 2024). It is hence recommended for practicing social workers to integrate trauma-informed perspectives into their assessments and interventions.

In summary, psychosocial assessment and the use of the bio-psycho-social-spiritual model provide a methodical framework for holistically assessing and examining a client's needs, resources, potential, and vulnerabilities in a range of areas and life domains. It is an important step and typically takes place before case planning and service implementation and delivery; however, it might also occur at different stages throughout direct practice with clients. It is the goal of case management to tie these different tasks and processes together in a coherent way, which will be discussed in the following section.

3.5 The Process of Case Management

The concept of case management originated from the concept of support management. It focuses on individualized care and tailored wrap-around support and assistance for a particular problem situation. The overall aim of case management is to provide individual and wrap-around care and to make the best possible use of (oftentimes limited) resources (Wendt, 2018). The linking of different tasks, objectives, and goals is an essential function of the case management process, as is the guidance of clients through the various help and support systems by means of subprocesses and concepts (DGCC, 2020; NCMN, 2009).

Contrary to the traditional individual casework model of social work, case management might be used when people face complex problems that require the involvement of several actors (service providers) acting together within a cooperative process. Psychosocial CVE interventions usually involve complex problem situations, requiring several systems to ideally work together, such as housing, education, mental health, justice/law, and so forth, so that the use of case management is necessary in nearly all cases (Walkenhorst et al., 2020). Indeed, recent research has confirmed the utility of case management in CVE, pointing to strengths and barriers for successful implementation of case management while underscoring that the effectiveness of case management tools in CVE is currently, at least from a research standpoint, poorly understood (Lewis et al., 2024).

3.5.1 Steps and Guiding Principles

Case management is a structured and planned approach designed to guide individuals toward positive outcomes within complex health and social circumstances and environments (DGCC, 2020; NCMN, 2009). Guided by the client's right to self-determination, this process can be described as composed of six critical steps, each underpinned by sub-processes and guiding principles to ensure effectiveness and client-centered care (NCMN, 2009). In practice, case management might be less of an orderly process and more of a spiral, with frequent returns to prior phases for clarification or a reworking of various tasks and activities (Sheafor & Horejsi, 2006). Case management has also received critique as well, which will be explored further below. The following six phases provide an idealistic scenario to how case management might unfold.

The first step is **identification and referral**. Individuals who may be at-risk of engaging in, or who are espousing violent extremism, are identified and referred to a CVE intervention program, and their eligibility for services is determined. This typically involves collaboration with various stakeholders and referral sources often including law enforcement, social services, probation/correctional officers, community organizations, schools, and mental health professionals. Oftentimes, parents or caregivers can also reach out when they are concerned about their child's behavior. Clients might, albeit rare, also self-refer. In general, criteria for referral may include attitudinal or behavioral indicators and prior or ongoing involvement in extremist activities, groups, or movements. Challenges may arise with certain referral pathways, however. For example, law enforcement might request information about a client referred into a psychosocial CVE program (e.g., request for detailed client progress updates), while social workers and other health care professionals are typically restricted by their codes of ethics to share protected information to ensure client privacy and integrity. Referrals might also be the result of multi-agency and community-building efforts, where the CVE intervention provider partakes in formalized (e.g., roundtables, multi-agency community conferences) or informal inter-agency collaboration.

Following identification, the next step is **intake and assessment**. The assigned caseworker might meet the client in the community, at an office, a correctional facility, or by using media (e.g., phone call, text messaging). Typically, an intake form will be completed together with the client, an overview of the program will be provided and issues around confidentiality will be discussed. As discussed above, assessment involves a thorough and holistic evaluation of the individual's history, risks, needs, strengths, values, and challenges within a bio-psycho-socio-spiritual framework. Using ecomapping, biographical evaluations, strengths-based, trauma-informed, suicide assessment, and other such tools, the assessment phase considers biological, psychological, social, economic, environmental, and cultural factors that may contribute not only to the individual's vulnerability to violent extremism but also to areas of resilience. Assessment might also include society-centered risk assessment for violent extremism to gauge the potential for harm toward both the client themselves and society. Assessment should be a reoccurring or ongoing process to assess change over time. Referring a client out for a clinical assessment, such as for psychiatric diagnosis, might also be important when the client presents with a mental illness or mental health-related symptoms. Part of the assessment process is the case formulation (see below). The guiding principles at this stage stress the importance of a holistic and strengths-based approach, recognizing the complex interplay of factors that contribute to extremism and focusing on the individual's vulnerabilities that can be addressed and strengths that can be leveraged in their intervention plan.

Case formulation is the critical bridge between assessment and intervention and it is being recognized as a critical component for assessment and intervention in CVE (Logan, 2023). It involves synthesizing the data collected during the assessment phase to create a coherent understanding of the individual's situation. This process reflects the social worker's interpretation of the client by using the bio-psycho-social-spiritual model, and it might be guided by the following **4 Ps model** (Bolton, 2014; Weerasekera, 2009)[9] which can be adapted to a CVE client context:

- *Predisposing Factors (Why me?)*: The factors that render an individual vulnerable to a particular problem or condition, such as engagement in violent extremism. In the context of CVE, this might include a history of trauma, social isolation, or initial exposure to extremist ideologies, peers, or content. It is important to note that "These factors increase the probability of a specific condition occurring if the specific factors prevail" (Weerasekera, 2009, p. 146).
- *Precipitating Factors (Why now?)*: The triggers that have led to a current crisis. For instance, a recent loss or a political event that triggered a grievance, experiencing bullying or social rejection, a recent arrest, or an encounter with an authority figure, that might have escalated the individual's involvement in or support for extremism.
- *Perpetuating Factors (Why does it continue?)*: These are the elements that maintain the problem over time and contribute to the longevity of the condition. They might include ongoing social-environmental stressors, such as continued exposure to extremist groups, exposure to violent extremist narratives or online hate, mis- or disinformation, but also complex psychosocial issues like prolonged substance abuse, ongoing family trauma, or untreated mental health conditions which can exacerbate one's vulnerability over time.
- *Protective Factors (What can I rely on?)*: These are the strengths and resources that can be leveraged to counteract the problem. Identifying these factors is crucial for designing interventions that build on the individual's existing resilience, such as supportive relationships, prior successes in overcoming adversity, or strong community ties and role models.

[9] The 4 Ps model integrates different types of causation and draws on the biopsychosocial model that was first developed by George Engel in the 1970s. The latter emerged from clinical psychiatry and psychology, proposing that health and illness result from a dynamic interplay of biological, psychological, and social factors (Bolton, 2014).

The rationale behind this approach to case formulation is that, for any given problem or condition, multiple factors across the bio-psycho-social-spiritual continuum contribute to its development, maintenance, and outcomes. On a practical level, case formulation offers an explanatory framework for why an individual presents with a particular issue, or a multitude of issues, at a specific time, emphasizing the importance of addressing a range of interacting variables. Typically, it reflects the language of a hypothesis and it ought to include an indication of the range, depth, and quality of the evidence it is based upon. As treatment progresses and new information becomes available, the case formulation should be revisited and, if necessary, revised to reflect a more accurate and evolving understanding of the client's situation (Logan, 2023; Weerasekera, 2009).

The third step is **case planning** (or intervention planning). Drawing on the information gathered from assessment and case formulation, this task involves creating a detailed plan that outlines specific, measurable short-, medium-, and long-term SMART goals[10] and the strategies and actions for how to achieve the client's goals. However, the case plan must be flexible to adapt to changes in the individual's circumstances and should involve the client in the decision-making process to ensure their active participation. Using approaches such as Motivational Interviewing (MI) are especially helpful in situations where clients see little or no value in pro-social goals or values. Since there may sometimes be friction when the client disagrees with pro-social goal setting, MI and Cognitive Behavioral Therapy approaches can help identify how clients' current context, beliefs, or behaviors are harming them as a way to instill a cognitive opening toward pro-social goals. Forming a trusting therapeutic alliance with their clients, practitioners might achieve this by focusing on meeting tangible basic needs and goals such as accessing housing, employment, food security, and so forth, to ensure the foundational tenets of social reintegration of their clients. During the case planning and implementation stage, it is worth remembering that social reintegration and multi-systemic interventions have yielded positive results and research confirms that interventions addressing several issues within the client's social ecology show positive effects in increasing resilience and protective factors against violent radicalization pathways (Lösel et al., 2018; Hassan et al., 2021a, 2021b). In other words, achieving pro-social goals is not a prerequisite for support and access to different services, but it could be a long-term goal for the client. The principles guiding case planning emphasize client self-determination, an individualized approach tailored to the unique needs, risks, and strengths of the client, as well as collaboration involving input from other stakeholders. MI therefore offers a methodological bridge between client ambivalence and goal-oriented action, and while already standard in corrections, MI is becoming increasingly relevant in CVE (*see below*). Case planning should also consider difficulties and challenges that might be encountered and how to overcome them (Logan, 2023).

---

[10] SMART is an acronym and stands for: specific, measurable, achievable, relevant, and time-based goals and goal-setting.

Fourth, once a case plan has been established, the next step is **implementation**. This involves putting the case plan into action by sequencing and coordinating services, making referrals, providing direct support (e.g., counseling, psychotherapy, psychoeducation, case advocacy, ongoing assessments), and continuously monitoring the client's progress. Navigating and building systems of belonging, as well as providing referrals, may sound straightforward, but they are often quite challenging in practice. For example, case managers need to acquire knowledge of community-based and specialized agencies and service providers in the area, including wait times and intake routines. As such, time and energy are necessary for practitioners to learn about resources and keep up with constant change in community programming—including staff turnover, change in programs, and so forth. This also involves educating other agencies about radicalization and its drivers and factors involved, primarily to reduce stigmatization about the client population, encourage service access, build capacity, and enhance inter-agency collaboration. Building systems of belonging might involve working with family members, other caregivers, or community partners, which requires family-based intervention and community development skills.

Clients may experience feelings of distress, distrust, or be triggered during the referral process, perhaps due to meeting new and unfamiliar persons, fear of stigmatization and service refusal, or other barriers (e.g., lack of financial support). Indeed, recent research suggested that "post-exit distress" and mental health challenges, including self-harm and suicidality, can arise during the processes of disengagement and reintegration—affecting areas such as daily life, basic needs, well-being, safety, identity, and life transitions (Meredith & Horgan, 2024). Consequently, the case manager must be prepared to anticipate and address these challenges, collaborating with the client to develop solutions to these barriers. Effective implementation relies on seamless coordination and trust among service providers, including mental health services, social services, community programs, and law enforcement if necessary. As Sheafor and Horejsi (2006, p. 61) emphasized:

> The case manager makes regular and frequent follow-up contacts with both the client and the service provider[s] to ensure that the needed services are actually received and properly utilized by the client. If not, action is taken to correct the situation or modify the service plan. [...] The case manager places emphasis on coordinating the clients' use of resources by becoming a channel and focal point for interagency communication.

The guiding principles here focus on coordination and responsiveness, ensuring that the client receives comprehensive care and that the plan can be adjusted as needed to address emerging issues. These principles are also aligned with the **Risk-Need-Responsivity** (RNR) Model[11] of case management and treatment that is considered best practice in corrections contexts (Andrews, 2011; Bonta & Andrews, 2007; Dyck et al., 2018).

[11] The RNR Model was first developed in the 1980s as the correctional field sought to shift from punishment to rehabilitation. The model has evolved to inform actuarial, professional judgment assessments, and treatment assignment that address a client or parolee's *risk* to reoffend, criminogenic *needs*, and what kind of treatment they are most likely to *respond* to successfully.

Evaluation is an ongoing process that assesses the effectiveness of the case management process and the client's progress toward their immediate and long-term goals and successes (outcomes). Individualized rating scales can be found online (Bringhurst et al., 2006) or created together with the client to measure timely indicators of the client's experience. For instance, developing a scale in which the client's status on a continuum from negative to positive functioning can be used at the beginning of each session or meeting. This can include using a point system representing the client's experience from best to worst or most to least, ranging between *1 to 10 points* for instance, and including negative points, such as *−1*, *−2*, as needed. This data allows for the visualization of evidence of change and progress in achieving identified goals (increases and decreases) over time. Co-creating the data also centers client agency and ownership of the service over time. Standardized evaluation forms and assessment tools, such as standardized rating scales, risk assessment tools for involvement in violent extremism, or suicide risk assessment, can be used at various points during the case management process to continuously measure and monitor client functioning and well-being over time (McKenzie & O'Brien, 2024). They do not come without challenges either, and social workers should determine if the measurement tool is appropriate with the client's cultural or age group (Sheafor & Horejsi, 2006). The principles guiding the evaluation stage are transparency, accountability, ensuring that interventions meet the client's needs, and that resources are used effectively, all while focusing on measurable outcomes.

Finally, the final **transition** step involves moving the client from intensive case management to a lower level of support, or to the termination of the intervention plan and services provision once the client's goals are met and there is no need for further services due to reduced risk factors and increased protective factors. This step ensures that the client has access to ongoing support systems, such as community organizations, other family members, or peer networks, to maintain positive outcomes in clients. The guiding principles here emphasize sustainability, focusing on building the client's capacity to maintain their progress independently, and empowerment, ensuring that the client has the skills and resources needed to continue their journey without intensive support. Typically, clients are welcome to contact the agency after termination if they are in need for support or help. Indeed, some programs expect that clients will return as progress is non-linear and reversions should not be stigmatized.

3.5.2 Case Management Competencies, Critique and Challenges

Case managers and practitioners working in CVE require both a broad and specialized competence profile to effectively support individuals in their journey away from violent extremist attitudes and behaviors. Key areas of competence include professional self-image, professional competence, methodological and procedural competence, social skills, and self-competence (DGCC, 2020). This is underscored by Rousseau et al. (2022) who proposed a three-pronged service model for extremist clients that includes: (1) multiple access points where clients can access therapy rapidly through different online and offline avenues, (2) specialized and trained care teams that have access to frequent supervision, and (3) collaborative integration of community services and programming to ensure long-term client support.

Professional self-image involves understanding one's role and maintaining ethical and social justice standards, and this is particularly important when supporting individuals who may have previously engaged in harmful activities. Professional competence encompasses deep knowledge of radicalization processes, risk and needs assessment, and intervention approaches and skills relevant for CVE, such as trauma-informed, family- and strengths-based approaches as well as case management. Methodological and procedural competence includes the ability to design, implement, and evaluate tailored intervention plans, utilizing evidence-based approaches while adapting them to the individual needs of the client.

Social skills are critical as they enable case managers to build trust, communicate effectively, and manage complex relationships between clients, their families, and other community stakeholders as well as mental health and human services providers. This competence is essential in creating a supportive and engaged environment that fosters disengagement. Finally, self-competence, self-care, clinical supervision, and social support for practitioners, which involve self-reflection, emotional resilience, and the ability to manage one's biases and emotional reactions, are vital when dealing with the emotionally charged and challenging cases often found in violent extremism; the role of critical thinking is also important when dealing with information, especially as social workers support clients in their own reflection and decision-making processes (Rousseau et al., 2022).

These competencies align with the multifaceted roles case managers should adopt, often acting as mediators, counselors, planners, guides, supporters, or advocates for their clients. As put by Sheafor and Horejsi (2006, p. 61):

> During the time services are being provided by the various recourses, the case manager assists the client and his or her family as they confront the inevitable problems in obtaining the desired services. This activity includes resolving personality conflicts, counseling, providing information, giving emotional support, and, when appropriate, advocating on behalf of clients to assure that they receive the services to which they are entitled.

Understandably, even the most seasoned and skilled social workers will be worn down by the complex and emotionally exhausting demands of this field. Effective case management in this context requires a high degree of emotional intelligence and professional adaptability, enabling case managers to navigate the complex and often challenging dynamics of disengagement from violent extremism.

However, case management as an intervention method has received a considerable amount of criticism. Case management has been described as too mechanical, paperwork-heavy and as a cost-cutting strategy, and when case management does not include advocacy strategies and ethical practice, it can be subject to reinforcing disempowerment and paternalism (Spindel, 2020). Relatedly, the lack of a grounding philosophy or ethics is another point of contention, and where case management is not grounded in client empowerment and social justice principles, social workers might work as enforcers of power-over and control mechanisms.

When it comes to CVE, as discussed in Chap. 1, there have been instances where social workers acted in and promoted securitization logics. Another point of concern is the traditional focus on the clients' problem areas and the stigmatizing impacts of labeling. If we only ask what is wrong with people and not what is right with them and if we do not transcend problems into needs, then we neglect centering on equally, if not more, important elements such as client strengths, optimism, agency, and gratitude and ultimately undermine "develop[ing] resilience during the times life becomes difficult" (Spindel, 2020, p. 31). There is a real need to focus on capabilities, client empowerment, and independence, "as we may inadvertently, and even with the best of intensions, actually disempower the people with whom we work by stressing our 'expert' role and the power of our knowledge" (Spindel, 2020, p. 19). Against this backdrop, client resistance should perhaps be best interpreted as a warning signal or function within the practitioner–client relation that something is currently not working. Oftentimes, that "something" is the professional's attempt to impose their own agenda and goals onto the client, and the client is resisting against it (Spindel, 2020). In complex case management, we often work with individuals with wounded self-esteem and hopelessness, and it is necessary to reacquaint clients with what is good about them, what is positive in their lives, and to build hope by marshalling their strengths and resources to address current problems and propel them toward a preferred future.

Relatedly, client testimonials and research have found instances where clients disengaging from violent extremism were faced with stigmatization practices and labeling, which might even include from social workers and psychosocial professionals themselves (United Nations Office on Drugs and Crime, 2016). This can have several negative consequences such as service denial, reduced self-esteem, self-doubt, reduced trust in others, and reinforced grievances or anger. This underscores once again the need for a non-judgmental, professional attitude paired with clinical principals such as trauma-informed care. As argued by Sheafor and Horejsi (2006, p. 75):

> The need to treat each and every client with respect and acceptance does not imply approval of all behavior by a client. One can accept and care for the client with dignity without approving of, for example, illegal, harmful, or socially destructive behavior [and/or ideologies]. The key to adhering to this principle is to remember that the purpose of social work is to help people make changes, and it has been amply demonstrated that acceptance of and respect for the person are prerequisite for change and that condemnation and judgementalism erect barriers to such change.

3.6 Clinical Practice and Intervention

3.6.1 Clinical Interventions

Therapeutic intervention or clinical practice can be a key element of case management, including in CVE. Typically facilitated by licensed and trained practitioners, including social workers, clinical intervention utilizes evidence-based psychosocial treatment approaches and modalities to provide specialized mental health care to clients and mitigate specific symptoms. In general, clinical practice is aimed at improving clients' mental, social, and emotional functioning, well-being and health by supporting them to better understand and navigate their feelings, modify unhelpful behavioral patterns, and learn how to cope with difficult circumstances in their social environments (Sheafor & Horejsi, 2006). Clinical social work often involves providing therapeutic support to clients over a specified period of time and it can include assessment, diagnosis of mental disorders (in some jurisdictions), short- or long-term mental health counseling, psychotherapy, and group and individual work. A differentiation can be made between counseling and psychotherapy; however, as these terms are often used interchangeably yet they differ in focus, depth, and purpose. There is considerable overlap between the two and it is beyond this chapter to provide a detailed discussion on how they differ. In short, psychotherapy, which can be performed by graduate-level social workers in some countries/jurisdictions including Canada, is typically focused on exploring deeper, more complex past experiences and associated underlying causes and unconscious patterns. Psychotherapy can be long-term, lasting months to years, as it often involves exploring complex and deeply rooted issues. On the other hand, counseling tends to focus on more immediate or situational challenges and practical solutions. Counseling is often shorter term than psychotherapy, lasting from a few sessions to a few months depending on the concern. Counseling is not typically focused on diagnosing, assessing, and treating mental illness.

An agency or program may have any combination of the abovementioned interventions and those discussed below, plus novel, organization-specific ones not discussed here. An underlying logic must weave every program activity and output together toward outcomes that are helpful to clients and the community. Logic models are a valuable resource to help staff, outside observers, and other stakeholders understand the *how, what,* and *why* of a program. There are several formats to choose from (Rubin & Babbie, 2016). Albeit non-exhaustive, what follows is an overview of relevant clinical intervention frameworks for supporting clients engaged in violent extremism.

Relationship and Rapport Relationship in social work practice might be thought of as an exchange at the emotional level and a dynamic interaction between persons in a professional setting (Heinonen & Spearman, 2001). This relationship connects people in a mutual process, typically resulting in rapport and trust between social worker and client. Social workers and other psychosocial professionals have a clear responsibility to establish a supportive relationship, guided by ethics, values, boundaries, legal statutes, and theory. In a purposive way, the social worker's *use of self* is a feature of the therapeutic relationship. *Use of self* refers to practitioners integrating and using their personal attributes, such as personality traits, belief systems, life experiences, positionalities, and cultural backgrounds, with their professional knowledge, values, and skills in order to build rapport and facilitate support for clients. The social worker's utilization of the use of self enables them to engage authentically and genuinely with clients, fostering effective relationships. By consciously applying aspects of themselves and upholding bias-sensitivity and critical reflexivity, social workers can better empathize with clients and tailor interventions to meet individual needs. The establishment of this kind of rapport is guided by purpose for both the client and the social worker. For instance, it is likely that the client's main purpose in establishing a relationship with a social worker is to gain access to certain resources or seek help in making changes in their lives. On the other hand, if the social worker is able to establish a caring and empathic relationship, then the helping process will more likely be effective as it will be built on a mutual relationship. Decades of research has shown that therapeutic rapport between the clinical social worker and the client is much more important than the specific therapeutic modality or approach used by the clinician; rapport in the therapeutic relationship is, in fact, *the most* reliable predictor of successful therapeutic outcomes for clients (McCoyd et al., 2022). At times, social workers and CVE practitioners must put effort into "non-clinical" interactions such as informal coffees, text messages, or recognizing holidays. Research on CVE practitioners speaks to the importance of such interactions to build trust within the context of their wider interventions (Cherney et al., 2022; Haugstvedt, 2019). Some people might wonder why social workers should support clients who have been engaged (or perhaps continue to being part of) violent extremist trajectories that cause harm. Understanding that radicalization is driven by vulnerability, lack of belonging, and unmet needs along the bio-psycho-social-spiritual continuum establishes the baseline to view clients holistically, empathically, and from a needs-based perspective. However, supporting those that espouse hatred and hostility toward others does not entail sympathizing with or validating their harmful views, behavior, and attitudes. Social workers instead try to understand and explain, *not excuse and justify*, clients' ideological constructions of themselves, others, and harmful behaviors. Practitioners typically attain this by being respectful, non-judgmental, working to understand the client as a product of their environment and histories, upholding do-no-harm principles, communicating with integrity and honesty with clients, maintaining confidentiality and privacy, and working to support clients' needs and well-being. These are all foundational elements of therapeutic rapport (Sheafor & Horejsi, 2006).

Understanding Social Labeling Establishing relationships with involuntary clients, such as justice-involved mandated clients, unwilling clients, and clients that do not trust social workers and other professionals, is not an easy task (Heinonen & Spearman, 2001). Social labeling, meaning the way others react to the label and how this reaction affects the client, is a process commonly known to those (formerly) involved in violent extremism. Given that most involuntary and unwilling clients have experienced labeling, we can use labeling theory in clinical settings to unpack such processes and stigmatization (Heinonen & Spearman, 2001). While Heinonen and Spearman (2001, p. 125) discussed labeling outside of social work practice within a CVE context, their assessment offers an important reflection for this field:

> if the labeling was perpetrated by the professional helpers, as frequently happens, this often helps explain some of the problematic behaviors of clients and why clients do not want help. Assessment must include a clear understanding of the social labeling process (not just the tag) and a clear understanding of how it affects clients.

Clients in their disengagement and exit journeys away from violent extremism are often faced with labeling practices from other psychosocial or helping professionals due to the stigma that is associated with violent extremism. Commonly, clients also face stigmatization and labeling from media sources and law enforcement who, for example, announce their release from correctional institutions back into the community. In such cases, communities sometimes experience a fear-based moral panic which can further stigmatize clients as well. Rousseau et al. (2022) showed that clients espousing violent extremism can be viewed as "unmotivated" and "scary," often experiencing service refusal from mental health practitioners. This can be triggering for such clients and reinforce reactive, maladaptive behaviors or their grievances and mistrust toward others. Do-no-harm and trauma-informed care principles become ever more relevant when supporting clients navigating social services, but also when educating other professionals about radicalization and disengagement and what their role might be within multi-agency settings.

Trauma-Informed Care Trauma-informed care or practice is an essential framework within social work and has also been applied to CVE. Many individuals drawn to extremist ideologies or milieus may have histories of trauma, such as adverse childhood experiences (ACEs), exposure to violence (e.g., family violence, child abuse), war, discrimination, or significant loss in combination with other contextualized hardships (e.g., histories of bullying, lack of social skills, chronic social isolation, and lack of belonging; Marsden & Lewis, 2021). In other words, subscribing to and engaging in violent extremism might sometimes be a maladaptive trauma response, and it hence becomes the work of the social worker to explore this impact across the bio-psycho-social-spiritual continuum (Marsden et al., 2024). From a socio-ecological perspective, research has found that the impacts of trauma at the individual level are often rooted in historical and/or contemporary social or collective experiences; similarly, individual radicalization pathways are oftentimes rooted in lived or perceived collective experiences and narratives. Trauma-informed care emphasizes understanding the impact of trauma and repeated experiences of trauma, including intergenerational trauma, on psychological, physiological, and behavioral outcomes, and ensuring that interventions do not inadvertently retraumatize the client or trigger the client's behaviors and cognitions. The principles of trauma-informed care, as outlined by Butler et al. (2011), include recognizing how past trauma can influence current behaviors and coping strategies, and prioritizing recovery from trauma by making the healing process a primary goal of clinical intervention. Trauma-informed care focuses on strengths, empowerment, and client control to ensure that clients have agency in their recovery process which might be achieved through a relational collaboration by means of a trusting and respectful relationship between the social worker and the client. This also includes creating a safe and respectful environment by ensuring that the service environment and other community agencies understand and respect the client's need for safety, acceptance, and cultural identity. Involving clients in service design by soliciting client input in the creation and evaluation of services is important to ensure services are responsive to their needs and minimize retraumatization by being mindful of how relations and interventions are delivered to avoid triggering past trauma.

Strengths-Based Practice The strengths approach is not a unified theory; rather, it might be best understood as a collection of ideas, approaches, and theories of practice (Heinonen & Spearman, 2001). Typically, social workers practicing from a strengths-based perspective engage clients with the intent to help them solve problems and increase their capacity through empowerment and building on their existing capacities, which might include, as argued by feminist, radical and structural theories, forms of personal agency, collective action, and community organizing to address social injustices. The central position of the strengths-based approach is to grow as human beings, improve quality of life, develop problem-solving and decision-making skills, and address stress and adversity (Heinonen & Spearman, 2001). Related to the strengths approach is empowerment, with the latter underscoring that power and capacity cannot be given by others. Social workers' role, then, is to encourage and support the inner strengths (power-within) and collective strengths (power-with) of clients so that, to the best of their ability, they take control of their own lives in pro-social ways (Heinonen & Spearman, 2001). In essence, the strengths approach is focused on self-determination and to meet this goal, this approach capitalizes on people's capacities, vitality, abilities, talents, courage, and power, seeing the client in charge of the helping process. Already being applied within CVE, strengths-based approaches provide an alternative or complimentary measure to risk or deficit thinking, grounding interventions in client's goals and values while focusing on skills and opportunities that help produce alternative meanings in order to pursue socially legitimate means (Stanley & Guru, 2015).

Systemic Counseling and Systems Thinking A similar strengths-based approach for CVE, although theorized and implemented differently, was put forward by Taubert (2021) who examined the *key-client model* in a CVE program, housed within the German nongovernmental organization called Legato. The key-client model is largely based on systems theory; as put by Taubert (2021):

> Radicalisation is always related to, and happens within, a social system. Whoever calls the helpline is part of that social system and carries multiple possibilities to change the system. Any change in behaviour or communication by a person who is part of the system sets other changes in motion and thus is able to influence radicalisation processes.

Building on client-centered, strengths-based, and systems theory, much of Legato's approach is focused on counseling and guiding the *key-client* such as social workers, youth workers, probation officers, teachers, parents, and caregivers instead of the individual radicalized to violence, the latter referred to as the *index-client*. According to Taubert, CVE counselors at Legato establish a trusting relationship with key-clients and work on their reflection, communication, and emotional skills and capabilities. The goal is to support behavioral change and new communication skills in key-clients in order to influence and invert radicalization processes of index-clients. How to build reliable relationships, positive emotional messages, and social acknowledgment are three areas of desired outputs and outcomes key-clients ought to acquire and implement within their ongoing and current relationship with the index-client. This type of work does not come without challenges, however. Oftentimes parents, as well as other professionals, are emotionally unprepared to change their own cognitive, behavioral, and communication patterns due to anger, certain dogmatic beliefs, lack of understanding, denial, or neglect. Feelings of guilt might arise due to past deconstructive influence on their children, or key-clients perceive their impact as less impactful and meaningless. Overall, this model supports different social systems represented via the key-client relationship aimed at influencing and deterring radicalization pathways in a social-constructive way (Taubert, 2021). The general systems perspective in social work reminds practitioners that usually there are several different types of intervention that can help client systems to change (Sheafor & Horejsi, 2006). For instance, in CVE it seems crucial that key-clients, such as teachers, become a meaningful part of the index-client's (for example, a teenager) social system by increasing positive engagement and communication with the index-client. This may result in change or adjustments in the youth vis-à-vis feedback generated through meaningful interactions with the teacher. Viewed from a systems perspective, disengagement can therefore be understood as a transformative process that includes input (taking in information), operations (using input and converting it into actions that can be applied), outputs (interactions with other systems), and feedback (processes to monitor its own functioning and making adjustments to maintain a steady state). In addition, family group conferencing is another model that centers the family system to discuss concerns and prioritize interventions from within the family or by drawing on local resources (*see* Chap. 4).

Motivational Interviewing Motivational interviewing (MI), increasingly used with clients who use substances, clients in correctional contexts, and with mandated clients who may be resistant to change (Clark, 2019; Sheafor & Horejsi, 2006; Wahab, 2005), has been recommended for application in CVE interventions (Clark, 2019; McKenzie & O'Brien, 2024). MI was proposed as an alternative model for facilitating increased buy-in for intervention and behavior change, and it has been recommended for utilization in different social work fields (Wahab, 2005). Originally developed by Miller and Rollnick, MI can be understood as a client-centered and directive method for enhancing intrinsic motivation for change by exploring and resolving ambivalence (Wahab, 2005). Understanding change as a multi-step process, this model rests on the observation that persons tend to be more committed to a treatment plan when they perceive it to be one of their own choosing and one that will sustainably address their personal concerns (Sheafor & Horejsi, 2006; Wahab, 2005). A key goal of MI in CVE contexts is to strengthen the client's sense of self-efficacy—that is, their belief in their ability to disengage and sustain change—by affirming their agency and reinforcing incremental successes throughout the process. CVE practitioners play a critical role in this work by using MI techniques to elicit and amplify the client's own reasons for change, thereby fostering confidence, motivation, and a stronger sense of ownership over their exit journey. Part of MI is to support clients to move along a continuum of behavior change (precontemplation, contemplation, preparation, action, maintenance, and relapse) by developing a supportive, non-judgmental, and directive environment to facilitate the exploration of one's motivations, readiness, confidence, and ambivalence levels for behavior change (Wahab, 2005). The intention behind assessing motivation, readiness, confidence, and ambivalence levels for change is to tailor the intervention so that it responds to the client's stage within the change continuum at any given moment. Rollnick and Miller underscored that it is the client's task to articulate and resolve ambivalence and it is the practitioner's role to support the client to explore and examine ambivalence further (Wahab, 2005). For instance, "an individual who is ready and motivated to change their behavior and does not feel confident that they can carry out the change, will require different supports and resources than if their barrier resides in their motivation level" (Wahab, 2005, p. 47). Clark argued that CVE practitioners should become knowledgeable about the behavior change process aiming to evoke and activate cognitive openings in clients and readiness for change. Using listening skills, reflective questioning, and engagement strategies, MI helps CVE practitioners centering on assessing and understanding readiness, confidence, and ambivalence instead of jumping to the problem-solving stage in situations where motivation and decision-making about change are still unknown or unclear (Clark, 2019).

Cognitive Behavioral Therapy and Dialectical Behavioral Therapy Given that violent extremist clients often follow harmful thought patterns and consequent behaviors, Cognitive Behavioral Therapy (CBT) and Dialectical Behavior Therapy (DBT) can play significant roles in intervention work to address underlying cognitive factors contributing to violent extremism. CBT and DBT are sometimes, though not always, used in tandem to target client's thought-behavior-emotional regulation patterns. CBT emphasizes the interconnectedness of thoughts, feelings, and behaviors, focusing on how they influence one another. While DBT addresses these aspects as well, its primary emphasis lies in emotional regulation, mindfulness, and accepting pain as a normal element of life. CBT aims to equip individuals with the skills to identify problematic thought patterns and redirect them effectively while, in contrast or perhaps in complement, DBT focuses on fostering self-acceptance, creating a sense of safety, and developing strategies to manage and tolerate emotions, ultimately helping individuals regulate behaviors that may be destructive or harmful. Through CBT and DBT, this combination of evidence-based modalities has particular efficacy with clients involved in violent extremism, since they can work to challenge and reframe problematic worldviews, manage emotional distress, dissuade pro-criminal ideologies or attitudes, change problematic behavior (toward themselves, i.e., self-harm, or toward others), and ideally lower recidivism (Altier et al., 2014; Broyd et al., 2022; Carlson, 2021; Horgan & Braddock, 2010).

3.6.2 Referrals for Psychiatric Examination

Clients involved in violent extremism frequently present with mental health challenges and while it is crucial to note that having mental health challenges or a psychiatric disorder does not cause violent extremism, it is very likely that undiagnosed and unmanaged mental health challenges can exacerbate and worsen one's alignment with violent extremist ideologies and behaviors (Rousseau et al., 2022; Trimbur et al., 2021). In these cases, clients should be referred for psychiatric examination (diagnosis) when they present with thoughts and behaviors that indicate mental illness, an undiagnosed mental condition, or a neurological disorder, and it is the task of the case manager to connect the client to appropriate services and professionals. As previously mentioned, some licensed clinical social workers have the capacity to formally diagnose mental disorders in clients, depending on the jurisdiction they work in. Some CVE intervention programs have established inter-agency agreements with mental health services, and the client's informed consent is necessary to make a referral for diagnosis. This is especially important in the context of CVE, where clients may fear being turned away from community-based and clinical services due to the stigma associated with violent extremism, as discussed in Chap. 1, resulting in the *bracketing off* practices by services and professionals not working in CVE directly but unaware of their critical role to support disengagement. CVE programs might also hire a clinical, psychological, or psychiatric professional on a contract basis if they do not have these services available in-house.

As well, in order to work and communicate in tandem with mental health agencies, social workers are tasked to use mental health terminology and classifications, typically those outlined in the Diagnostic and Statistical Manual of Mental Disorders (DSM), and to use diagnosis for clinical treatment planning and evidence-based interventions. However, there are several problems associated with the DSM such as the focus on clients' pathologies, including false positives, what constitutes as evidence, cultural considerations, and diagnostic labels. Further, from a person-in-environment lens, social workers in general should, as discussed throughout this chapter, provide holistic assessments and interventions which encompass psychological functioning but also social functioning, strengths, and coping strategies. It is worth remembering that the DSM is a classification system of mental disorders, not a classification of people (Sheafor & Horejsi, 2006).

3.7 Conclusion

In the field of countering violent extremism, we see a steady increase of social work theory and practice utilized to describe, design, implement, and evaluate disengagement interventions aimed at those at-risk of or already engaged in violent radicalization trajectories. This chapter explored key theories and intervention modalities including case management and clinical approaches, and discussed the complexities of assessment and intervention processes. Using common theories and approaches including case management, trauma-informed practice, and social work's bio-psycho-social-spiritual model, this chapter laid the foundation of how disengagement from violent extremism can be accomplished within multi-sectoral and social work-led contexts. Emerging evidence in secondary and tertiary CVE programs furthermore underscored the need to situate CVE more firmly within social work, and, as argued by several scholars and discussed in this book, to view clinical or psychosocial CVE as an emerging and new field of social work practice. For social work researchers, this presents the unique opportunity to tap into a new and relevant area of practice. Empirical priorities now include validating integrative assessment procedures and testing case management across settings. Questions such as, how clinical CVE compares to other social work and violence prevention fields, including preventing gender-based violence, street-level/gang violence, and sexual violence, are worth exploring, as well as questions focused to examine the challenges and ethical dilemmas faced by frontline practitioners working in clinical CVE. Building off this chapter, the next chapter (Chap. 4) will provide an overview of key issues in clinical CVE settings, such as multi-sectoral collaboration and ethics, working with minors and family members, and CVE in correctional and criminal justice contexts.

References

Altier, M. B., Thoroughgood, C. N., & Horgan, J. G. (2014). Turning away from terrorism: Lessons from psychology, sociology, and criminology. *Journal of Peace Research, 51*(5), 647–661. https://doi.org/10.1177/00223433145359

Andrews, D. A. (2011). The risk-need-responsivity (RNR) model of correctional assessment and treatment. In J. A. Dvoskin, J. L. Skeem, R. W. Novaco, & K. S. Douglas (Eds.), *Using social science to reduce violent offending* (pp. 127–151). Oxford University Press. https://doi.org/10.1093/acprof:oso/9780195384642.003.0039

Awan, I. (2012). 'I am a Muslim not an extremist': How the prevent strategy has constructed a 'suspect' community. *Politics & Policy, 40*(6), 1158–1185. https://doi.org/10.1111/j.1747-1346.2012.00397.x

Baaken, T., Korn, J., Ruf, M., & Walkenhorst, D. (2021). Dissecting Deradicalization: Challenges for theory and practice in Germany. *International Journal of Conflict and Violence (IJCV), 14*, 1–18. https://doi.org/10.4119/ijcv-3808

Barrelle, K. (2015). Pro-integration: Disengagement from and life after extremism. *Behavioral Sciences of Terrorism and Political Aggression, 7*(2), 129–142. https://doi.org/10.1080/19434472.2014.988165

Berzoff, J. (2011). Why we need a biopsychosocial perspective with vulnerable, oppressed, and at-risk clients. *Smith College Studies In Social Work, 81*(2–3), 132–166. https://doi.org/10.1080/00377317.2011.590768

Birdsey, N., & Kustner, C. (2021). Reviewing the Social GRACES: What Do They Add and Limit in Systemic Thinking and Practice? *The American Journal of Family Therapy, 49*(5), 429–442. https://doi.org/10.1080/01926187.2020.1830731

Bjørgo, T., & Horgan, J. G. (2008). *Leaving terrorism behind: Individual and collective disengagement*. Routledge.

Bogo, M. (Ed.). (2018). *Social work practice: Integrating concepts, processes, & skills*. Columbia University Press.

Bolton, J. W. (2014). Case formulation after Engel—The 4P model: A philosophical case conference. *Philosophy, Psychiatry, & Psychology, 21*(3), 179–189. https://doi.org/10.1353/ppp.2014.0027

Bonta, J., & Andrews, D. A. (2007). *Risk-need-responsivity model for offender assessment and rehabilitation (User Report No. 2007–06)*. Public Safety Canada.

Bringhurst, D., Watson, C., Miller, S., & Duncan, B. (2006). The reliability and validity of the outcome rating scale: A replication study of a brief clinical measure. *Journal of Brief Therapy, 5*(1), 23–30.

Brouillette-Alarie, S., Hassan, G., Ousman, S., Laetitia Savard, É., Kilinc, D., Madriaza, P., Varela, W., Pickup, D., & Danis, E. (2025). Systematic review on the outcomes of tertiary prevention programs in the field of violent radicalization. *Journal for Deradicalization, 42*, 140–193. https://journals.sfu.ca/jd/index.php/jd/article/view/1027/515.

Broyd, J., Boniface, L., Parsons, D., Murphy, D., & Hafferty, J. D. (2022). Incels, violence and mental disorder: A narrative review with recommendations for best practice in risk assessment and clinical intervention. *BJPsych Advances, 29*(4), 1–11. https://doi.org/10.1192/bja.2022.15

Burns, A., Dannecker, E., & Austin, M. J. (2018). Revisiting the biological perspective in the use of biopsychosocial assessments in social work. *Journal of Human Behavior, 29*(2), 177–194. https://doi.org/10.1080/10911359.2018.1500505

Butler, L., Critelli, F., & Rinfrette, E. (2011). Trauma-informed care and mental health. *Directions in Psychiatry, 31*, 197–210.

Buttner, P., Gahleitner, S. B., Hochuli Freund, U., & Röh, D. (2018). Soziale Diagnostik. Eine Einführung. In P. Buttner, S. B. Gahleitner, U. Hochuli Freund, & D. Röh (Eds.), *Handbuch Soziale Diagnostik. Perspektiven und Konzepte für die Soziale Arbeit* (pp. 11–30). Lambertus.

Campelo, N., Oppetit, A., Thompson, C., Cohen, D., & Louet, E. (2022). A clinical and psychopathological approach to radicalization among adolescents. *Frontiers in Psychiatry, 13*, 788154. https://doi.org/10.3389/fpsyt.2022.788154

Ceylan, R., & Kiefer, M. (2018). *Radikalisierungsprävention in der Praxis: Antworten der Zivilgesellschaft auf den gewaltbereiten Neosalafismus*. Springer VS. https://doi.org/10.1007/978-3-658-15254-3

CPN-PREV. (2025). *The state of validation of tools that assess risk for violent extremism. A Systematic Review Summary Pamphlet.* Canadian Practitioners Network for the Prevention of Extremist Violence.

Carlson, L. (2021). *The role of psychotherapy in rehabilitation and exit work.* Radicalisation Awareness Network. Retrieved March 11, 2025, from https://home-affairs.ec.europa.eu/system/files/2021-11/ran_role_of_psychotherapy_in_rehabilitation_and_exit_work_112021_en.pdf.

Cherney, A. (2018). Evaluating interventions to disengage extremist offenders: A study of the proactive integrated support model (PRISM). *Behavioral Sciences of Terrorism and Political Aggression, 10*(2), 103–120. https://doi.org/10.1080/19434472.2018.1495661

Cherney, A., De Rooy, K., & Williams, R. (2022). An evidence review of strategies targeting youth who have radicalised to violent extremism. *Journal for Deradicalization, 33*, 40–69. https://journals.sfu.ca/jd/index.php/jd/article/view/667/385

Chivers, C. (2018). 'What is the headspace they are in when they are making those referrals?' Exploring the lifeworlds and experiences of health and social care practitioners undertaking risk work within the prevent strategy. *Health, Risk & Society, 20*(1–2), 81–103. https://doi.org/10.1080/13698575.2018.1437121

Clark, M. D. (2019). Motivational interviewing for deradicalization: Increasing the readiness to change. *Journal for Deradicalization, 20.* https://journals.sfu.ca/jd/index.php/jd/article/view/245/169.

Clemmow, C., Fowler, N., Seaward, A., & Gill, P. (2025). Risk of what and why? Disaggregating pathways to extremist behaviours in individuals susceptible to violent extremism. *Behavioral Sciences & the Law, 43*(3), 228–247. https://doi.org/10.1002/bsl.2710

Clesle, A., Knäble, J., & Rettenberger, M. (2024). Risk and threat assessment instruments for violent extremism: A systematic review. *Journal of Threat Assessment and Management.* https://doi.org/10.1037/tam0000223

Corner, E., & Pyszora, N. (2022). The terrorist radicalization assessment Protocol-18 (TRAP-18) in Australia: Face validity, content validity, and utility in the Australian context. *Journal of Policing, Intelligence and Counter Terrorism.* https://doi.org/10.1080/18335330.2022.2117993

Custodial Institutions Agency. (n.d.). *European Database of Terrorist Offenders.* Retrieved July 9, 2025, from https://www.vera-2r.nl/research/eu-database.

Dechesne, M. (2011). Deradicalization: Not soft, but strategic. *Crime, Law and Social Change, 55*(4), 287–292. https://doi.org/10.1007/s10611-011-9283-8

DGCC - Deutsche Gesellschaft für Care und Case Management. (2020). *Case Management Leitlinien—Rahmenempfehlungen, Standards und ethische Grundlagen.* medhochzwei Verlag.

Duits, N., & Kempes, M. (2023). Interrater and intra-rater reliability of the VERA-2R tool. *Frontiers in Psychiatry, 14*, 1236295. https://doi.org/10.3389/fpsyt.2023.1236295

Dyck, H. L., Campbell, M. A., & Wershler, J. L. (2018). Real-world use of the risk-need responsivity model and the level of service/case management inventory with community-supervised offenders. *Law and Human Behavior, 42*(3), 258–268. https://doi.org/10.1037/lhb0000279

Eisenman, D., Weine, S., & Lashley, M. (2020). Can public health help prevent violent extremism? Should public health help prevent violent extremism? In S. von Hlatky (Ed.), *Countering violent extremism and terrorism. Assessing domestic and international strategies* (pp. 47–63). McGill-Queen's University Press.

El-Mafaalani, A., Alma, F., Mansour, A., Müller, J., Nordbruch, G., & Waleciak J. (2016). *Ansätze und Erfahrungen der Präventions- und Deradikalisierungsarbeit.* Leibniz-Institut Hessische Stiftung Friedens- und Konfliktforschung.

Feddes, A. R. (2015). *Socio-psychological factors involved in measures of disengagement and Deradicalization and evaluation challenges in Western Europe*. Middle East Institute.

Figlestahler, C., & Schau, K. (2020). *Entwicklungen, Handlungspraxen und Herausforderungen im Feld der Ausstiegs- und Distanzierungsarbeit. Wissenschaftliche Begleitung Handlungsbereich Land im Bundesprogramm "Demokratie leben!" in der Förderphase 2020 bis 2024. Schwerpunktbericht DJI.* Deutsches Jugendinstitut. Retrieved March 11, 2025, from https://www.dji.de/fileadmin/user_upload/DemokratieLeben/Schwerpunktbericht_2020_%20Ausstiegs-_und_Distanzierungsarbeit.pdf.

Finn, J. L. (2021). *Just practice. A social justice approach to social work.* Oxford University Press.

Fischer, J., & Dunn, K. (Eds.). (2019). *Stifled Progress – International Perspectives on Social Work and Social Policy in the Era of Right-Wing Populism.* Verlag Barbara Budrich. https://doi.org/10.2307/j.ctvfrxr60

Gill, P., Marchment, Z., Seaward, A., Doherty, P., & Goodman, K. (2023). How can general violence risk assessment and management inform that of violent extremist risk? In J. Busher, L. Malkki, & S. Marsden (Eds.), *The Routledge handbook on radicalisation and countering radicalisation* (pp. 476–497). Routledge. https://doi.org/10.4324/9781003035848-35

Grossman, M., Ungar, M., Brisson, J., Gerrand, V., Hadfield, K., & Jefferies, P. (2017). *Understanding youth resilience to violent extremism: A standardised research measure. Final research report.* Alfred Deakin Institute for Citizenship and Globalisation, Deakin University. https://doi.org/10.13140/RG.2.2.21022.79689

Grossman, M. (2021). Resilience to violent extremism and terrorism. In M. Unger (Ed.), *Multisystemic resilience* (pp. 293–317). Oxford University Press. https://doi.org/10.1093/oso/9780190095888.003.0017

Miramahdi, H. (2016). Building resilience against violent extremism: A community-based approach. *The Annals of the American Academy of Political and Social Science, 668*(1), 129–144. https://doi.org/10.1177/0002716216671303

Hassan, G., Madriaza, P., Brouillette-Alarie, S., Danis, E., Varela, W., Ousman, S., Kilinc, D., Savard, É. L., Lavoie, L., & The CPN-PREV Team. (2022a). *Guidelines for the prevention of violent extremism online and offline: Findings from the expert conference and the Delphi consensus process.* Canadian Practitioners Network for the Prevention of Radicalization and Extremist Violence. Retrieved March 11, 2025, from https://cpnprev.ca/guideline-committees.

Hassan, G., Brouillette-Alarie, S., Ousman, S., Madriaza, P., Varela, W., Danis, E., Kilinc, D., Pickup, D., Borokhovski, E., & CPN-PREV team. (2022b). PROTOCOL: Are tools that assess risk of violent radicalization fit for purpose? A systematic review. *Campbell Systematic Reviews, 18*, e1279. https://doi.org/10.1002/cl2.1279

Hassan, G., Brouillette-Alarie, S., Ousman, S., Savard, É. L., Kilinc, D., Madriaza, P., Varela, W., Pickup, D., Danis, E., & The CPN-PREV Team. (2021a). *A systematic review on the outcomes of tertiary prevention programs in the field of violent radicalization.* Canadian Practitioners Network for the Prevention of Radicalization and Extremist Violence. Retrieved March 11, 2025, from https://cpnprev.ca/systematic-review-3/.

Hassan, G., Brouillette-Alarie, S., Ousman, S., Kilinc, D., Savard, É. L., Varela, W., Lavoie, L., Fetiu, A., Harris-Hogan, S., Borokhovski, E., Pickup, D., Madriaza, P., Rousseau, C., Thompson, S. K., McCoy, J., Venkatesh, V., Boivin, M., Srimathi Narayana, M., Morin, D., &… The CPN-PREV Team. (2021b). *A systematic review on the outcomes of primary and secondary prevention programs in the field of violent radicalization.* Canadian Practitioners Network for the Prevention of Radicalization and Extremist Violence. Retrieved March 11, 2025, from https://cpnprev.ca/systematic-review-2/.

Haugstvedt, H. (2019). Trusting the mistrusted: Norwegian social workers' strategies in preventing radicalization and violent extremism. *Journal for Deradicalization, 19*, 149–184. https://journals.sfu.ca/jd/index.php/jd/article/view/219/159.

Heath-Kelly, C. (2017). The geography of pre-criminal space: Epidemiological imaginations of radicalisation risk in the UK prevent strategy, 2007–2017. *Critical Studies on Terrorism, 10*(2), 297–319. https://doi.org/10.1080/17539153.2017.1327141

Heinonen, T., & Spearman, L. (2001). *Social work practice. Problem solving and beyond.* Irwin Publishing.

Horgan, J., & Braddock, K. (2010). Rehabilitating the terrorists? Challenges in assessing the effectiveness of de-radicalization programs. *Terrorism and Political Violence, 22*(2), 267–291. https://doi.org/10.1080/09546551003594748

Horgan, J. (2014). *The psychology of terrorism* (2nd ed.). Routledge.

Irwin, N. (2015). The complexity of responding to home-grown terrorism: Radicalisation, de-radicalisation and disengagement. *Journal of Policing, Intelligence and Counter Terrorism, 10*(2), 166–175. https://doi.org/10.1080/18335330.2015.1089639

Khalil, J., Horgan, J., & Zeuthen, M. (2019). The attitudes-behaviors corrective (ABC) model of violent extremism. *Terrorism and Political Violence, 34*(3), 425–450. https://doi.org/10.1080/09546553.2019.1699793

King, M., St-Amant, M., & Doering, S. (2025). *Measuring progress in a CVE program: A 3-year longitudinal case study. Full Report.* CREST. Retrieved February 19, 2026, from https://crest-research.ac.uk/resources/measuring-progress-in-a-cve-program-a-3-year-longitudinal-case-study/

Koehler, D. (2016). *Understanding Deradicalization. Methods, tools and programs for countering violent extremism.* Routledge.

Kolbe, A. R. (2019). Do home-based social work services increase the success of programming to prevent violent extremism: Evidence from a small-scale intervention in an urban east African population. *Clinical Research in Psychology, 2*(2), 1–6. https://asclepiusopen.com/clinical-research-in-psychology/volume-2-issue-2/5.pdf

Kupfer, A. (2018). Netzwerkkarten als diagnostische Instrumente. In P. Buttner, S. B. Gahleitner, U. Hochuli Freund, & D. Röh (Eds.), *Handbuch Soziale Diagnostik. Perspektiven und Konzepte für die Soziale Arbeit* (pp. 320–327). Lambertus.

Lewis, J., Marsden, S., Cherney, A., Zeuthen, M., Rahlf, L., Squires, C., & Peterscheck, A. (2024). Case management interventions seeking to counter radicalisation to violence and related forms of violence: A systematic review. *Campbell Systematic Reviews, 20*, e1386. https://doi.org/10.1002/cl2.1386

Lloyd, M., & Dean, C. (2015). The development of structured guidelines for assessing risk in extremist offenders. *Journal of Threat Assessment and Management, 2*(1), 40–52. https://doi.org/10.1037/tam0000035

Lösel, F., King, S., Bender, D., & Jugl, I. (2018). Protective factors against extremism and violent radicalization: A systematic review of research. *International Journal of Developmental Science, 12*(1–2), 89–102. https://doi.org/10.3233/DEV-170241

Lowrance, W. W. (1980). The nature of risk. In R. C. Schwing & W. A. Albers (Eds.), *Societal risk assessment—how safe is safe enough?* (pp. 5–17). Springer US.

Logan, C. (2023). From behaviours to people: Formulation-based risk management in violent extremism. In C. Logan, R. Borum, & P. Gill (Eds.), *Violent extremism: A handbook of risk assessment and management* (pp. 135–177). UCL Press. https://doi.org/10.14324/111.9781800081970

Logan, C. (2021). *Violent extremism: The assessment and management of risk.* CREST Security Review, 16–19. Retrieved August 24, 2025, from https://crestresearch.ac.uk/comment/violent-extremism-the-assessment-and-management-of-risk/.

Marsden, S., & Lewis, J. (2021). *Trauma, Adversity, and Violent Extremism. Full Report.* CREST. Retrieved July 9, 2025, from https://crestresearch.ac.uk/resources/trauma-adversity-and-violent-extremism/.

Marsden, S., Lewis, J., & Leslie, A. (2024). *Trauma, adversity and violent extremism. Implications for Risk Assessment. Full Report.* CREST. Retrieved March 11, 2025, from https://crestresearch.ac.uk/resources/trauma-adversity-and-violent-extremism-implications-for-risk-assessment/.

McCoyd, J. L. M., Curran, L., Candelario, E., & Findley, P. (2022). "There is Just a Different Energy": Changes in the therapeutic relationship with the telehealth transition. *Clinical Social Work Journal, 50*(3), 325–336. https://doi.org/10.1007/s10615-022-00844-0

McKenzie, A., & O'Brien, D. (2024). The evolution of estimated time of arrival: The city of Toronto's CVE program. *Journal for Deradicalization, 39*, 94–128. https://journals.sfu.ca/jd/index.php/jd/article/view/911

Meloy, J. R., & Gill, P. (2016). The lone-actor terrorist and the TRAP-18. *Journal of Threat Assessment and Management, 3*(1), 37–52. https://doi.org/10.1037/tam0000061

Meloy, J. R., & Roshdi, K. (2021). Operationalizing the terrorist radicalization assessment Protocol-18 (TRAP-18) for threat assessment. *Behavioral Sciences & the Law, 39*(3), 257–273. https://doi.org/10.1002/bsl.2483

Meredith, K., & Horgan, J. (2024). After they leave: Exploring post-exit distress in former violent extremists. *Journal for Deradicalization, 38*, 165–210. https://journals.sfu.ca/jd/index.php/jd/article/view/865/465

Morrison, J. F., Silke, A., Maiberg, H., Slay, C., & Stewart, R. (2021). *A systematic review of post-2017 research on disengagement and deradicalisation*. CREST. Retrieved January 30, 2026, fromhttps://crestresearch.ac.uk/resources/a-systematic-review-of-post-2017-research-on-disengagement-and-deradicalisation

Mücke, T. (2016): *Zum Hass verführt. Wie der Salafismus unsere Kinder bedroht und was wir dagegen tun können*. Eichborn.

NCMN. (2009). *Canadian standards of practice for case management*. National case management network. Retrieved March 11, 2025, from https://campusmentalhealth.ca/wp-content/uploads/2018/03/Canadian-Case-Management-Standards-of-Practice.pdf.

Ohlenforst, V., Ruf, M., Selby, A., Swidziniewski, A., Ünal, Ö., & Walkenhorst, D. (2022). *DISLEX 3D - Distanzierungsprozesse im islamistischen Extremismus: Eine systematisierende Erhebung der Parameter zur Selbst- und Fremdbeobachtung in drei Dimensionen. Abschlussbericht.* Modus Zad. Retrieved March 11, 2025, from https://modus-zad.de/wp--content/uploads/2022/11/2022-modus-insight_DISLEX-3D-4.pdf.

Paternoster, R., & Bushway, S. (2009). Desistance and the feared self: Toward an identity theory of criminal desistance. *Journal of Criminal Law & Criminology, 99*(4), 1103–1156.

Pressman, E. D., & Flockton, J. S. (2016). Calibrating risk for violent political extremists and terrorists: The VERA 2 structured professional judgment approach. *The International Journal of Forensic Mental Health, 11*(1), 66–80. https://doi.org/10.1080/14999013.2016.1166464

Pressman, E. D., & Flockton, J. S. (2012). Calibrating risk for violent political extremists and terrorists: The VERA 2 structured assessment. *The British Journal of Forensic Practice, 14*(4), 237–251. https://doi.org/10.1108/14636641211283057

Rabasa, A., Pettyjohn, S. L., Ghez, J. J., & Boucek, C. (2010). *Deradicalizing Islamist extremists*. RAND Corporation. Retrieved March 11, 2025, from http://www.rand.org/pubs/monographs/MG1053.html

Ragazzi, F. (2017). Countering terrorism and radicalisation: Securitising social policy? *Critical Social Policy, 37*(2), 163–179. https://doi.org/10.1177/0261018316683472

Reisch, M. S. (2019). Social work under Trump: Experiences from the USA. In K. Dunn & J. Fischer (Eds.), *Stifled progress: Social work and social policy in the era of right-wing populism* (pp. 147–166). Verlag Barbara Budrich.

Rousseau, C., Frounfelker, R., Ngov, C., & Crocker, A. (2022). Clinical services addressing violent extremism: The Quebec model. *International Journal of Forensic Mental Health, 22*(3), 222–232. https://doi.org/10.1080/14999013.2022.2147254

Rousseau, C., Johnson-Lafleur, J., Ngov, C., La Rochelle, X., Brouillette-Alarie, S., Gignac, M., Veissière, S., & Crocker, A. (2024). Risk assessment challenges in a specialized clinic for individuals referred for violent extremism. *Journal of Threat Assessment and Management, 11*(2), 67–82. https://doi.org/10.1037/tam0000214

Rubin, A., & Babbie, E. (2016). *Research methods for social work* (9th ed.). Cengage.

Ruf, M., & Walkenhorst, D. (2021). *The potential of social diagnostics for P/CVE*. Radicalisation Awareness Network.

Scarcella, A., Page, R., Furtado, V., & Abe, T. (2016). Terrorism, radicalisation, extremism, authoritarianism and fundamentalism: A systematic review of the quality and psychometric properties of assessments. *PLoS One, 11*(12). https://doi.org/10.1371/journal.pone.0166947

Sheafor, B., & Horejsi, C. R. (2006). *Techniques and guidelines for social work practice*. Pearson.

Sjøen, M. M. (2020). *When counterterrorism enters the curriculum. Exploring risks and practices of the securitization of education (PhD thesis)*. University of Stavanger.

Stanley, T., & Guru, S. (2015). Childhood radicalisation risk: An emerging practice issue. *Practice, 27*(5), 341–356. https://doi.org/10.1080/09503153.2015.1053858

Stanley, T., & Barracosa, S. (2024). Responding to radicalisation and extremism risk for youth: An emerging child protection and youth justice practice issue in Aotearoa. *Aotearoa New Zealand Social Work, 36*(3), 83–88. https://doi.org/10.11157/anzswj-vol36iss3id1161

Spindel, P. (2020). *Case management from an empowerment perspective. A guide for health and human services professionals* (4th ed.). Canadian Scholars.

Taubert, A. (2021). *The key-client model*. RAN Practices. Retrieved March 11, 2025, from https://home-affairs.ec.europa.eu/networks/radicalisation-awareness-network-ran/collection-inspiring-practices/ran-practices/key-client-model_en.

Thomas, P. (2018). Changing but still controversial: The UK's "Prevent" strategy. In J. Kargel (Ed.), *"They have no plan B." Radicalization, departure, return – Between prevention and intervention* (pp. 129–138). Bundeszentrale für politische Bildung.

Trimbur, M., Amad, A., Horn, M., Thomas, P., & Fovet, T. (2021). Are radicalization and terrorism associated with psychiatric disorders? A systematic review. *Journal of Psychiatric Research, 141*, 214–222. https://doi.org/10.1016/j.jpsychires.2021.07.002

Ungar, M. (2013). Resilience, trauma, context, and culture. *Trauma, Violence, & Abuse, 14*(3), 255–266. https://doi.org/10.1177/1524838013487805

United Nations Office on Drugs and Crime. (2016). *Handbook on the management of violent extremist prisoners and the prevention of radicalization to violence in prisons*. UN Office on Drugs and Crime.

van der Kolk, B. (2014). *The body keeps the score: Brain, mind, and body in the healing of trauma*. Penguin Books.

Wahab, S. (2005). Motivational interviewing and social work practice. *Journal of Social Work, 5*(1), 45–60. https://doi.org/10.1177/1468017305051365

Walkenhorst, D. (2022). Fragmentierung und Entkopplung: Warum im Feld der Distanzierungsarbeit kein systematischer Erfahrungs- und Wissensaustausch stattfindet—und was dagegen getan werden kann. *Unsere Jugend, 74*, 172–180.

Walkenhorst, D., Baaken, T., Ruf, M., Leaman, M., Handle, J., & Korn, J. (2020). *RAN rehabilitation manual—rehabilitation of radicalised and terrorist offenders for the first line practitioners*. Radicalisation Awareness Network. Retrieved March 11, 2025, from https://home-affairs.ec.europa.eu/networks/radicalisation-awareness-network-ran/publications/rehabilitation-manual-rehabilitation-radicalised-and-terrorist-offenders-first-line-practitioners_en.

Weerasekera, P. (2009). A formulation of the case of Antoinette: A multiperspective approach. In P. Sturmey (Ed.), *Clinical case formulation: Varieties of approaches* (pp. 145–156). Wiley. https://doi.org/10.1002/9780470747513.ch11

Weilnböck, H., & Uhlmann, M. (2018). *20 Thesen zu guter Praxis in der Extremismusprävention und in der Programmgestaltung*. Bundeszentrale für politische Bildung. Retrieved March 11, 2025, from https://www.bpb.de/themen/infodienst/264235/gute-praxis-in-der-praevention/.

Wendt, W. R. (2018). *Case Management im Sozial- und Gesundheitswesen: Eine Einführung*. Lambertus.

Wolf, K. (2019). Wie können Wirkungen pädagogischer Interventionen gemessen werden? In M. C. Begemann & K. Birkelbach (Eds.), *Forschungsdaten für die Kinder- und Jugendhilfe* (pp. 395–423). Springer VS.

Wolfowicz, M., Litmanovitz, Y., Weisburd, D., & Hasisi, B. (2021). Cognitive and behavioral radicalization: A systematic review of the putative risk and protective factors. *Campbell Systematic Reviews, 17*, e1174. https://doi.org/10.1002/cl2.1174

Yuzva Clement, D., Kiefer, J., Hassan, G., & King, M. (2022). Countering radicalization to violence in Canada: A multi-sector perspective. In R. Ceylan & M. Kiefer (Eds.), *Der islamische Fundamentalismus im 21. Jahrhundert: Analyse extremistischer Gruppen in westlichen Gesellschaften* (pp. 325–345). Springer VS. https://doi.org/10.1007/978-3-658-37486-0_16

Chapter 4
Special Issue Areas and Opportunities

4.1 Introduction

Countering violent extremism (CVE) now relies on multi-sectoral collaborations among social work, education, mental health, spiritual guidance or mentorship, law enforcement, corrections, and so forth. This chapter emphasizes the critical role of such collaboration in CVE efforts, particularly as these initiatives expand to include diverse sectors and disciplines. Multi-sectoral or multi-agency collaboration involves strengthening resource development and capacity building across various groups through coordinated efforts. However, these collaborations often face challenges that can hinder critical dialogue and learning.

The importance of multi-sectoral collaboration is further underscored when working with children and youth, especially those at risk of radicalization or whose parents are involved in extremism. Adolescents, who are navigating a tumultuous phase of self-discovery and identity formation, can be particularly vulnerable to radicalization due to their developmental stage, expanding social circles, and exposure to hateful and extremist content online including harmful engagement or grooming within virtual gaming communities. Additionally, this chapter explores the challenges and opportunities of working in prisons and correctional contexts. Social workers in these settings are tasked with navigating the complexities of practicing in punitive and securitized environments. Despite these challenges, prisons and correctional facilities can also serve as places for positive change, offering opportunities for multidisciplinary resourcing and programming. In summary, this chapter presents practical concepts, theoretical frameworks, and aims to offer a thorough understanding of how multi-sectoral collaboration can significantly enhance CVE efforts including in correctional contexts and when addressing youth radicalization.

D. Yuzva Clement et al., *Social Work and Countering Violent Extremism*, SpringerBriefs in Social Work, https://doi.org/10.1007/978-3-032-07086-9_4

4.2 Multi-Agency Collaboration: Challenges and Opportunities

With the emergence of psychosocial CVE efforts in many countries outside of the national security and law enforcement realm, there has been a simultaneous push for multi-agency and multi-sectoral collaboration. Multi-sectoral or multi-agency collaboration can be understood as “Strengthen[ing] collaborative resource development by and for practitioners across multiple sectors and disciplines through capacity building in areas of high need” (Hassan et al., 2021, p. 9). Others have defined multi-sectoral collaboration as “Developing a broad, comprehensive strategy that employs multiple preventive mechanisms and their pertinent measures instead of focusing on a narrower range of mechanisms and measures” (Bjørgo, 2016, p. 42). Social work scholarship has developed models and theories with regard to multi-sectoral or multi-agency collaboration most notably within the fields of community practice and child welfare (Regehr et al., 2016). For example, governed by law and ethics, there lies great responsibility in social workers “to use discretion in determining which cases should be referred [to child protection services] and which should not” (Regehr et al., 2016, p. 79). In many jurisdictions, professionals such as teachers and social workers have a clear legislative requirement to report suspected child abuse or neglect; however, research shows that sometimes frontline professionals fail to do so. Reasons for this behavior are complex, and reasons for non-reporting include “ethical considerations about confidentiality, lack of awareness regarding definitions of abuse, reluctance to appear in court, and frustrations regarding lack of feedback from child welfare services once a report is made” (Regehr et al., 2016, p. 87). Ensuring child well-being and safeguarding against harm depend on effective information sharing; however, “Sharing information can be problematic” (Regehr et al., 2016, p. 94). Seeking informed consent from the client, acting under a court order or legislation, or responding to emergency situations where consent is not required, highlights the varied contexts and scope in which confidentiality, privacy, and information disclosure are managed and addressed (Regehr et al., 2016). As the next few paragraphs will show, these complexities also receive considerable attention within CVE.

For instance, Sivenbring and Malmros (2019, pp. 31–32) assessed multi-agency collaboration for CVE in Nordic countries and highlighted

> the possibilities, problems and challenges that occur as agencies with different agendas and expertise come together. (…) In fact, internal conflicts in teams of professionals working together across institutional boundaries seem to be rather common.

Multi-agency and multi-sectoral collaboration can be challenging for frontline workers. Both more distant (Chivers, 2018; Stanley et al., 2017; van de Weert & Eijkman, 2019) as well as recent studies (Haugstvedt, 2022; Haugstvedt & Tuastad, 2023; Haugstvedt & Gunnarsdottir, 2023; Stanley & Barracosa, 2024; van de Weert & Eijkman, 2021; van de Weert, 2022; Yuzva Clement et al., 2022) have shown that multi-agency collaboration for CVE seems to be a reoccurring challenge for social workers and other psychosocial professionals which might result in uncertainty, stress, or ethical trespass. Collaboration with law enforcement and security agencies, for example, is often seen as a continuous area of tension, particularly regarding information sharing and in direct practice contexts. For example, suppose that a social worker was referred a radicalized client from a law enforcement agency. Although the spirit of collaboration might result in law enforcement officials inquiring about the client's progress, the legal confines of confidentiality might result in the social worker refusing to share these details. As mentioned, in many jurisdictions, social workers and other professionals are legally obligated to disclose information when required by law or court order, or when necessary to prevent serious, imminent, or foreseeable harm to service users or others. Against this backdrop, Berner, who differentiated between *security* and *safety*[1] concerning CVE, argued that the concept of safety allows social work and law enforcement "to meet at the same level, to define their tasks clearly, [but also] separately from each other" (Berner, 2022, p. 36). Reflecting on the risk of securitization in social work due to close proximity to law enforcement and its security-logic, Berner suggested for social work to adopt the concept of safety in order to promote positive outcomes for clients, social cohesion, and community well-being when working in collaborative spaces with law enforcement. Stanley and Barracosa (2024, p. 86) also discussed that responding to radicalization and violent extremism risk for youth can involve law enforcement services:

> we will be working together [with police and security services]. It is important that we appreciate the social work role as distinct from security services whilst also remaining collaborative. Our role is to undertake a comprehensive ecological assessment to understand the situation.

Collectively and in line with social work ethics, the abovementioned authors suggested for social workers to engage in transparent and ethical handling of information (e.g., being transparent about one's role, respecting client privacy and confidentiality, and obtaining client consent to share information), utilize and highlight social work approaches within multi-sectoral contexts, engage in joint trainings, team-building, and knowledge mobilization across groups and sectors, and provide peer-mentorship and supervision for social workers. Other challenges in multi-sectoral collaboration for CVE can include staff turnover, limited funding, ad-hoc collaboration models instead of long-term and stable models, as well as the absence of trust and legal frameworks for information sharing (Canadian Practitioners Network for the Prevention of Extremist Violence, 2024).

Building on case studies and data collected from a multi-agency violence prevention program that ran in a U.S. city and targeted youth at-risk of violence, including violent extremism, Ellis and colleagues found that local partners, such as law

[1] Berner (2022) viewed *security* as a broad, often political concept tied to economic capacity but also national values that could exclude and stigmatize minorities. In contrast, Berner referred to *safety* as individuals' personal, community-based, and psychological sense of protection and well-being.

enforcement, education, health and social services, took several steps to establish trust and work collaboratively as a team: time was reserved for monthly meetings to set goals and standards for collaboration and referral pathways, discuss service provision, as well as to have transparent discussions on professional's mandates, ethics, responsibilities, and roles (Ellis et al., 2022). A key topic in this process was to establish *information sharing protocols* especially with regard to the role and involvement with local and federal law enforcement agencies. It was made clear both to clients and community partners that only when there was imminent threat (to oneself or others) would social service providers share information with law enforcement (Ellis et al., 2022).

A similar approach was recently outlined by McKenzie and O'Brien (2024, pp. 108–109) regarding the Toronto-based psychosocial CVE intervention program called Estimated Time of Arrival (ETA); the authors outlined that

> Inter-agency trainings with law enforcement are important as ETA clients are often already interacting with or being monitored by police due to their risk to public safety. [...] Police and Yorktown ETA staff educate each other on their mandates, regular duties and common referral pathways. Key to these trainings is articulating how policing and Yorktown professionals handle participant information, explaining different laws and limitations that govern the sharing of information for each group of professionals, and particular pathways that will be used when information needs to be shared.

Ultimately, multi-agency collaboration largely involves what social work scholar Finn (2021) described as effective engagement and *teaching–learning* within and across organizations and groups. Finn (2021, pp. 247–248) highlighted that challenges can arise not only from differing personal, theoretical, and linguistic/conceptual lenses, but also from "power relations among professionals [which] must be named and made talkable. [...] Through critical dialogue, interprofessional team members can dislodge implicit assumptions, question their certainties, and open themselves to new learning." As seen with Ellis et al.' (2022) research, both time and effort were needed to put such recommendations into practice, and Finn underscored that teaching–learning is a collective strategy implicating everyone part of multi-agency or interprofessional teams or settings.

4.3 Youth Radicalization: Working with Youth and Families

The phenomenon of youth violent radicalization has recently received considerable amount of attention (Hutchinson et al., 2025; RCMP, 2024; Rousseau et al., 2024; Stanley & Barracosa, 2024). From a developmental perspective, adolescence can be understood as an often-stressful and turbulent period of identity negotiation and formation. As such, youth radical behavior should not automatically be equated with radicalization trajectories because adolescence and youth behavior are often coined by varying degrees of radicality, or *being radical* and *different*. Youth cultures, social movements spearheaded by young people, as well as youth peer group behavior, deviance, and risk-taking in general, are often coined by unconventional attitudes and social norms or behaviors as well as forms of political activism that challenge the status quo, including from an intergenerational standpoint (Lösel et al., 2018; Yuzva Clement, 2022). The questioning of mainstream social norms, calling for radical change in pursuit for social change and justice, as well as experimenting with and advocating for diverging social norms and ideas, is *coherent* with developmental stages during adolescence, from which processes of radicalization should be distinguished (Yuzva Clement, 2022).

There are a number of ways in which young people can be viewed, including the following: as *vulnerable*, arguing that youth are susceptible to dangers and risk; as *problems*, viewing youth as deviant and potentially harmful toward others and themselves; or as *consumers*, not fully ready to contribute to society and subject to marketing and entertainment (Erwin, 2016). Cleary, these categorizations all favor the deficit-based model of deviance or development centered around risk, moral panic, and simplistic understandings that adolescents are not as developed, and therefore not as self-aware, as their adult counterparts. However, when viewed as *co-creators* and from a strengths- and asset-based perspective, youth demonstrate the capacity to create, contribute, and to make an impactful difference (for example, through youth-led and youth-focused initiatives); therefore, youth ought to be empowered to be part of the solution and citizenry (Erwin, 2016; Yuzva Clement, 2022).

Nevertheless, young people can become vulnerable to pathways of violent extremism. A complex interplay of risk factors and unmet needs can increase the likelihood for some youth to engage in extremist online milieus, including the development and distribution of extremist content, and by means of threats or plans to engage extreme violence (RCMP, 2024; Stanley & Barracosa, 2024). Vulnerability toward radicalization and "violence-sustaining affects (e.g., anger, disappointment, resentment)" (Gheorghe, 2023, p. 59) might increase during adolescence as young persons undergo a complex journey of self-discovery and cultural identity formation, experience insecurity and emotional intensity while developing a need for independence, empowerment, peer group belonging, and autonomy (Erwin, 2016). Furthermore, delayed frontal cortical maturation is an important cognitive-developmental factor during adolescence (Campelo et al., 2022; Sapolsky, 2017). As such, adolescents are generally more susceptible to external influences, as the prefrontal cortex—responsible for executive functions such as impulse control, decision-making, and abstract reasoning—does not fully mature until around 24 to 26 years of age, increasing their sensitivity to reward signals, challenges with self-regulation, and vulnerability to social pressures (Casey et al., 2008; Sapolsky, 2017).

As such, adolescents are easily influenced and impressionable, increasing their susceptibility of being exploited and radicalized, especially online (Campelo et al., 2022; Gereluk, 2023; Rousseau et al., 2020). One should not, however, ignore the developing agency and capacity of young people, too. While many are "recruited" into online spaces, astute CVE practitioners should be open to the fact that some youth can also be active recruiters and amplifiers of hate, disseminating hate material and enlisting the support of peers. Motivations to recruit and radicalize others are diverse and can include status attainment, maladaptive coping strategies and responses to mental health challenges, ideological conviction, threat response, adventure/thrill seeking, and more.

However, as previously mentioned throughout this book, "creating a type of 'checklist' for signs of radicalization problematically suggests a certainty that has not been substantiated by any evidence of those who work in counterterrorism" (Gereluk, 2023, p. 439). Professionals, such as teachers, youth workers, and social workers, should refrain from labeling youth or surveilling their discussions and deliberations around (potentially controversial) ideological and political issues. Instead, they can create dialogic pedagogical spaces and, within formal education, a whole-of-school approach grounded in developing and implementing critical consciousness, inclusion, democratic principles, student engagement, and dialogue (Gereluk, 2023).

Still, extremist groups and actors use sophisticated techniques to exploit youths' cognitive and emotional traits, as well as their emerging agency, to manipulate and mobilize youth in favor of extremist community objectives and a sense of belonging. Joining an extremist group or movement, or following such groups or influencers online, can offer the sense of camaraderie, validation, or purpose in life that disenfranchised youth often seek. Indeed, extremist actors or environments engage what is referred to as *love bombing*, which is especially motivational for those youths experiencing social alienation, hopelessness, and discrimination. Extremist cultures are frequently portrayed as warm, welcoming, and even empowering to young people. Scholars have also highlighted a shift away from formal engagement to cultural and emotional participation in extremism or extremist milieus, due to the widespread utilization of visual artifacts such as meme culture, iconography, songs, lyrics, and aesthetics (Campion & Colvin, 2024; Gereluk, 2023).

Among a small subset of youth, researchers have found that youth suffering from depression and experiencing loneliness, abuse, and toxic stress (e.g., within family environments) mediated sympathy for violent radicalization, meaning that these particular intersections of cumulated mental health stressors and challenges and repeated exposure to extremist ideas or materials can increase vulnerability to radicalization and even legitimatize violent extremism (Campion & Colvin, 2024; Rousseau et al., 2020). Using a psychopathological approach, Campelo et al. (2022) examined a psychiatric sample of 20 youth with radicalization conduct and serious mental illness that received treatment in a psychiatric hospital in Paris, France. The authors found the recurrence of feelings of loneliness and school bullying before radicalization, as well as family dysfunction and early childhood psychological control issues exacerbated vulnerability (Campelo et al., 2022). Stabilizing psychiatric pathology, including through medication, was a successful intervention for some of the youth; other youth with extreme overvalued beliefs continued to pose a risk toward violence after psychiatric treatment, necessitating prolonged psychosocial and psychotherapeutic support:

> Our experience has shown the need for at least 1 year of educational and psychotherapeutic support to allow these adolescents to reflect on themselves and on their history, at which point they can eventually utilize the support offered to them. (Campelo et al., 2022, p. 17)

The online environment can exacerbate risk and vulnerability among youth. The omnipresence of online hate, violent extremist and terrorist content, as well as gore, imagery depicting harm, self-harm, injury, and suffering on social media including messaging boards, gaming platforms, and gaming-adjacent communities pose certain risks (Stanley & Barracosa, 2024). In fact, in a pan-European study of 9- to 16-year-olds ($N = 10,000$), participants reported a range of risks that concern them on the Internet (Livingstone et al., 2014). The researchers found that pornography (22%), cyberbullying (19%), and violent content (18%) were at the top of young people's concerns (Livingstone et al., 2014). The intersection between online gaming including gaming-adjacent communities and violent extremism has received considerable scientific attention lately (Koehler et al., 2023; Schlegel & Kowert, 2024). Research has stressed the role of personal relationships, emotional closeness, and the influence of trust on a person's cognitive openness toward radicalization (Schlegel & Kowert, 2024, p. 75):

> Recruitment in online games is functionally different from traditional forms of off- and online recruitment. As social, playful spaces, gaming environments can "emotionally jump-start" relationships between players, accelerating the formation of close, tight-knight interpersonal connections. In essence, a player may learn to trust someone much more quickly than they would in traditional, non-digital relationships, because of the presence of a shared, stressful activity.

As a result, interventions aimed at preventing and countering radicalization to violence have begun to unfold in gaming spaces. For example, a program in Germany reaches youth engaging with far-right narratives and content in gaming spaces through *one-to-many* outreach posts and *one-to-one* chat conversations, utilizing chat and networking functions of gaming-adjacent platforms; another example is Gamers for Peace, which is a community-led initiative aimed at creating inclusive and pro-social gaming spaces using livestreams, posting interviews and other video content distributed via YouTube, Twitch, and Discord. In the Netherlands and the United Kingdom, trust building and development of critical thinking skills takes place through police officers playing video games with young users (Schlegel et al., 2025).

Furthermore, recent research has examined how children under the age of 13 can also be exposed to online extremist content and susceptible to promoting extremist attitudes, ideas, and behaviors in schools and peer groups, oftentimes leaving teachers, frontline workers, and parents or caregivers wondering how to interrupt such trajectories (Hutchinson et al., 2025). For example, boys and young men are often drawn into the manosphere[2] not through an initial alignment with misogynistic

---

[2] The manosphere can be understood as a loosely affiliated network of different misogynistic digital platforms and communities that engage with controversial political, cultural, and social issues related to masculinity, gender, and the experiences of men and boys (Hutchinson et al., 2025). Examples include forums like Reddit's r/MensRights, incel communities, and male supremacist influencers on platforms like YouTube or X (formerly Twitter). While not inherently violent, some segments of the manosphere have been linked to an elevated risk of radicalization and gender-based violence.

ideologies, but rather through a search for guidance on issues such as dating, self-confidence, and personal development. These online spaces frequently present themselves as sources of practical advice or critiques of contemporary, diverse and inclusive gender norms, which can appear benign or even constructive at first glance. However, as users engage more deeply, they are gradually exposed to increasingly extremist content and influencers offering parasocial relationships that frame men as victims of systemic bias, particularly in relation to feminism and shifting social expectations (Hutchinson et al., 2025). This process of ideological escalation is often facilitated by algorithmic recommendation systems that prioritize engagement over nuance, thereby reinforcing polarizing narratives. Within manospheric digital communities, users find validation and a sense of belonging that can be especially compelling for those who feel socially isolated, disempowered, and lacking trusting relationships. Loneliness, in particular, acts as a powerful catalyst, making individuals more susceptible to the emotional appeal and group identity offered by these spaces. Over time, this environment can foster the internalization of male supremacist beliefs, effectively radicalizing individuals who may have initially sought support or self-improvement. Indeed, law enforcement and security agencies from Australia, Canada, New Zealand, the United Kingdom, and the United States have recently confirmed a rising trend of radicalization among youth and urged for a whole-of-society approach to address the risk of youth violent radicalization (RCMP, 2024):

> A renewed whole-of-society approach is required to address the issue of minors radicalising to violent extremism. This is not something governments or communities can address in isolation. Mental health, community initiatives, social services, and education interventions can help to counter radicalisation before security and policing responses are required.

The role of parents, guardians, and youth-serving organizations is especially pertinent. Psychoeducation can be a helpful approach for social workers when working with parents and guardians as well as other frontline professionals aimed at establishing a deeper and more nuanced understanding about the contextual experiences, vulnerabilities, and protective factors during childhood and adolescence. Social workers can offer psychoeducation to exemplify the relevance of cognitive, social, and emotional development with regard to factors such as emotional and behavioral dysfunction, adverse childhood experiences, susceptibility to peer pressure and risk-taking, family conflict and various forms of neglect, trauma, educational disconnect, feelings of alienation and hopelessness, adventure-seeking and desire for change, online dis/misinformation and hate as well as online safety and digital literacy more generally, and the impact of social isolation and mental health issues (Campelo et al., 2022; Stanley & Barracosa, 2024).

4.3.1 Family-Based Interventions

Next to psychoeducation, other scholars have put forth dialogic family-based intervention approaches to address youth radicalization within family contexts (Stanley et al., 2017; Stanley & Barracosa, 2024). Stanley and others have suggested using a strengths-based approach to risk thinking and to support the family unit to address safety concerns.

The *signs of safety* approach is a partnership model establishing the client-family system as the expert and deconstructing risk discourses that are harmful for clients (Stanley et al., 2017; Stanley & Barracosa, 2024). Here, risk is viewed as something that is fluid and flexible, which can then be managed. Through a 0–10 scaling system (0 meaning danger and 10 meaning safe enough), family members can engage in risk and safety interpretations alongside practitioners. This can also include an expansive ecomapping exercise (*see* Chap. 3) where digital communities and online spaces are jointly evaluated for their risks and strengths, pointing to digital nodes otherwise invisible to caregivers. There seems to be an urgent need for parents and caregivers (and other professionals) to advance their competence and skills in online safety and digital literacy, and social workers are well-placed to provide this type of psychoeducation. The power-sharing approach of signs of safety provides an opportunity for family dialogue, reflection on assets, strengths, protective factors, gaps, and needs. Family risk and safety interpretations and proposed solutions can then be used in assessment and treatment planning as part of case management. However, parental denial in response to children's harmful behavior and related family issues (e.g., trauma) remains a barrier to intervention and support. It might stem from fear, guilt, stigma, or certain parenting styles (e.g., permissive, neglectful), leading caregivers to minimize, avoid, or dismiss problematic behavior, which can delay support or worsen outcomes. Approaches to addressing parental denial might include building a sense of safety in caregivers, fostering open dialogue, enabling healthier parent–child dynamics, but perhaps also providing clinical intervention to parents or family members directly to address their psychological or emotional barriers. As discussed above, addressing youth radicalization typically involves multi-sectoral stakeholders such as parents and caregivers, educators, health and social service professionals, youth workers, and sometimes justice partners and law enforcement. If information sharing protocols are established and informed client consent is provided, the signs of safety model proposes that youth, their family, and surrounding professionals gather, collaboratively learn and discuss risk views and interpretations, reach an analysis about the degree of risk and protective factors, and collectively develop goals and next steps (Stanley & Barracosa, 2024).

Stanley et al. (2017) also highlighted the value of the *family group conference (FGC)* method as a promising approach to working with radicalization concerns. It originated in the child welfare system and is being practiced across many jurisdictions (Regehr et al., 2016). Grounded in restorative justice and empowerment approaches, this method provides a collaborative space for families to locate solutions and options to keep their children safer (Regehr et al., 2016). Notably, there is a process in which the family has confidential private time in which to dialogue and plan without the presence of any social service or security professional (Stanley et al., 2018). Similar to the signs of safety approach, FGC is a powerful and balanced antidote to the individualizing and silencing effects produced by securitized networks (Stanley et al., 2017). These authors also drew on the capability approach, introduced by Amartya Sen and Martha Nussbaum, to promote social justice and to shift the focus toward clients' ability to exercise formal rights. Differentiating between opportunities or means (capabilities) and outcomes (functioning), Stanley et al. (2018) showed how limited capabilities, including vulnerabilities and structural disadvantages, hinder achieving positive outcomes. This theory helps foster a multidimensional analysis and ethical decision-making for working with radicalization cases. These authors remind frontline practitioners working in multi-agency settings tasked with radicalization cases to use "tools and approaches that help us to work ethically and effectively as social workers (which) is our unique and important difference to other disciplines and agencies" (Stanley et al., 2018, p. 144).

While much focus has been on children radicalizing on their own accounts, another challenge is supporting children of extremist parents. Extremist organizations or groups can sometimes force certain value systems onto parents and subordinate them under rigorous parenting behaviors in adherence with in-group and ideology conformity, instilling fear and hostility as well as excessive devotion and loyalty in both parents and children (RAN, 2018; Rousseau et al., 2024; Schermaier-Stoeckl et al., 2018). Even without direct ties to such groups, families may still normalize extremist views, especially when other vulnerabilities—like domestic violence or mental health issues—are present, increasing children's risk of radicalization (Campion & Colvin, 2024). Extremist groups have also tried to influence schools by promoting hate, such as anti-trans or racist narratives, through local school board trustee elections (Canadian Anti-Hate Network, 2022).

Research has shown that children of extremist parents may experience loyalty conflicts toward their parents or the group (Schermaier-Stoeckl et al., 2018). Judgmental communication by professionals can worsen this, harming trust and the therapeutic relationship; trauma-informed, attachment-based training is needed for those working with such families (Rousseau et al., 2024; Schermaier-Stoeckl et al., 2018). A supportive school environment can act as a protective factor, especially when it is inclusive, non-judgmental, and connected to community resources. When engaging with extremist parents, focusing on children's rights, development, and school attachment can help build trust and encourage positive involvement (RAN, 2018).

Working with children and their extremist parents often involves working across sectors and domains. In this case, it might involve social work, child protection, medical professionals, law enforcement, justice, or security agencies. As viewed above, multi-sectoral collaboration is both an area of inter-agency learning but also an environment where tensions and conflict can arise. For example, psychosocial professionals might assess the relationship and attachment between a child and the child's extremist parents as positive or needing adjustment, and that separation would be harmful (Rousseau et al., 2024). Others have argued that transgenerational extremism and trauma could cause danger to the child; however, the parent's ideological conviction alone is often not sufficient legal ground to remove a child from its parents (RAN, 2019).

In terms of upstream prevention approaches, Hutchinson and colleagues suggested to prioritize digital media literacy in schools, promote community engagement, and engage in parental discussions about child safety online (Hutchinson et al., 2025). As well, by drawing on research regarding the correlation between student voice, recognition, and engagement in the classroom, Gereluk (2023) proposed a whole-of-school approach to tackle youth radicalization and highlighted the role of teachers to leverage their authenticity and ethos to create deliberative spaces for students to be present and heard, and to invite students to participate in critical conversations and reflections. Macro-level interventions ought to incentivize tech companies responsible for products used by children and youth to implement age verification, transparency, safety design, and advanced moderation policies, but also supporting localized cultural figures in the youth's lifestyle and development alongside social workers and childhood educators. While gaps remain in implementing effective strategies within educational and community settings, what has become clear is to engage child-, youth-, and family-serving organizations and functions, such as kindergartens, early childhood education, schools, community organizations, social services, child welfare organizations, and libraries, but also to provide social supports and communities of practice so that frontline workers enhance their own well-being, knowledge, and skill development (Gereluk, 2023; Hutchinson et al., 2025).

4.4 CVE in Correctional and Criminal Justice Contexts and the Role of Social Workers

As discussed throughout this book, social workers play a crucial role in multi-agency settings tasked with radicalization cases. Stanley et al. (2018) emphasized the importance of equipping social workers with tools and approaches that enable them to practice ethically and effectively—particularly when working with individuals involved in, or at risk of entering, the criminal justice system. They highlighted the distinct role of social work in this context, setting it apart from justice and enforcement-oriented approaches. Social workers practicing within correctional institutions or settings, as well as those working in community-based contexts supporting justice-involved clients, need advanced knowledge and skills to work with correctional partners. They must understand how to collaborate with multiple stakeholders, including mental health professionals and forensic psychologists, judicial systems, prison services, parole/probation services, law enforcement, intelligence services, families, and communities (Jakob et al., 2024). This multi-sectoral cooperation is crucial for providing comprehensive rehabilitation and social reintegration services.

Many individuals who adhere to a violent extremist ideology remain in the community because they have neither committed a crime nor indicated an imminent risk to public safety. Some of these individuals may self-desist, or are managed in the community through interventions or extra-judicial measures (i.e., diversion). Diversion occurs when an individual has committed a crime but is at low-risk to public safety and more likely to rehabilitate in the context of structured community supports than going through the process of conviction and sentencing. In the context of CVE, diversion has been used to support youth who have engaged in hate-based vandalism for instance. Restorative justice theory and practice is used to inform many diversion practices, and its emergent use in the context of hate crime is being studied (Gavrielides, 2012). Also, Canada has introduced "Terrorism Peace Bonds," which allow a provincial court judge—if convinced by the evidence that an individual poses a terrorist threat—to issue a court order requiring the person to keep the peace and be of good behavior for up to 12 months, and, in some cases, to undergo treatment (GOC, 2024). As such, given the emergence of criminal justice procedures that can mandate or encourage community-based measures, CVE programming must ensure it has a robust presence within the community and an ethics-grounded relationship with justice partners in order to meet clients in their locales and to ensure courts and other justice actors are well informed about available, appropriate, and effective services.

CVE programming might also unfold in prisons, as seen in some jurisdictions. Psychosocial CVE programs are met with numerous challenges that lie within prison systems, which can include overcrowding and reduced access to conditions that promote and protect physical and mental health (United Nations Office on Drugs and Crime, 2016). Prisons can also be potential locations for radicalization to violence, even for prisoners sentenced for offences unrelated to violent extremism.[3] At the same time, prisons can also provide an opportunity for disengagement from violent extremism and can function as a catalyst for positive change (United Nations Office on Drugs and Crime, 2016). A further challenge lies within correctional professionals that exhibit anti-democratic views and othering (Jakob et al., 2024). Positive interactions with correctional professionals who engage in humane and pro-social behavior toward violent extremist prisoners can create cognitive openings for changes in prisoners' thinking and behavior, thus providing the foundation for tailored programming and case management intervention which address unmet needs (Jakob et al., 2024; United Nations Office on Drugs and Crime, 2016).

One current challenge that has received increased attention over the past years is rehabilitation and social reintegration interventions for so-called returning foreign fighters (or extremist travelers), often referred to as *returnees*. Depending on the jurisdiction, these individuals might be charged upon arrival in their home country and placed in detention, and returning children might be placed into foster care or with extended family members. In other cases, returnees might be monitored without charges due to insufficient evidence of their involvement with a foreign terrorist entity. Several scholars emphasize the need for psychosocial CVE interventions for children returning from conflict zones like the former Islamic State/Daesh or prison

---

[3] To ensure that prison authorities can identify illicit activities, including activities related to violent extremism and terrorism, prisons typically have a structured intelligence system to collect security and related information. This is important to not only ensure the safe operation of prison facilities but also regarding the prevention of radicalization to violence. Prison intelligence structures can support and assist in intake, assessment and classification, and inform correctional programming as well as rehabilitative measures (United Nations Office on Drugs and Crime, 2016).

camps (Rousseau et al., 2024; United Nations Office on Drugs and Crime, 2016). The EU's former Radicalisation Awareness Network (RAN, 2021) highlighted the importance of comprehensive rehabilitation and reintegration interventions for such cases, recommending family-based, trauma-informed, and social reintegration approaches. The aim is to provide long-term mental health support, stabilize living conditions, advocate in schools, and enhance community belonging and health support for children and families.

Recognizing trauma is vital, especially for returning foreign fighters from conflict zones. While radicalization is not necessarily linked to mental disorders, these individuals often experience high levels of mental health issues. Trauma-informed care and mental health services are hence essential components of their rehabilitation. Alongside providing mental health services, social workers ought to support social reintegration processes. A strengths-based approach aims to support "individuals post-release to experience active participation in local communities and inclusion in functional systems key to successful reintegration after prison release" (Walkenhorst et al., 2020, p. 24).

As well, there is growing concern over the developing nexus of violent extremism and organized crime. Terrorist and criminal organizations both disregard the rule of law—albeit for different reasons—and may recruit from similar lower socioeconomic milieus. Terrorist organizations may finance their activities and gain operational capabilities through various illicit means such as drug trafficking or kidnapping for ransom, and leverage the informal or shadow economies of organized crime to funnel resources toward their areas of operation (Global Counterterrorism Forum, 2018; Global Initiative Against Transnational Organized Crime, 2024). CVE practitioners should be mindful of the potential overlap and the implications for treatment. Clients convicted of offenses that are seemingly unrelated to terrorism or violent extremism may still be appropriate referrals.

In other cases, individuals may be deeply committed to violence and engage in criminal activity that is ideologically, socially, and materially motivated. This nexus is increasingly visible in cases like the so-called Com/764 network, a decentralized transnational group that blends cybercriminal tactics, sexual extortion, child abuse, animal abuse, and ideological violent extremism. Emerging from several existing subcultures—including neo-Nazism and the violent militant accelerationist ecosystem—the most notorious group to arise from the Com is 764 (Argentino et al., 2024). Members of 764 have coerced youth into producing child sexual abuse material, committing acts of self-harm, and in some cases, even suicide. The group operates across online networks and gaming platforms such as YouTube, Discord, Roblox, and Telegram, targeting vulnerable youth through manipulation and grooming, often under the guise of friendship or romantic interest. According to researchers, several members who became abusers were initially victims themselves, perpetuating a cycle of trauma that fuels the community's growth and cohesion (Argentino et al., 2024). Such examples underscore the need for CVE practitioners to understand how ideological, social, and criminal motives can intersect, and to be equipped to respond to cases that may not fit traditional terrorism or extremism contexts but still pose serious risks to public safety, social cohesion, and child and youth well-being (Argentino et al., 2024; Smith, 2025).

As mentioned, psychosocial CVE efforts or programs can also take place within prison systems. In 2023, Jakob et al. (2023) published a study examining the challenges and opportunities faced by social workers employed in psychosocial CVE programs in German prisons. The study examined practitioners from civil society organizations providing direct services with groups and individuals in prisons and probationary services who were assessed as being at-risk of radicalization (e.g., those showing vulnerability toward radicalization but sentenced for drug trafficking and aggravated bodily injury for instance) and those sentenced for political violence and terrorism-related offenses. Social workers were faced with numerous challenges due to pedagogical paradoxes when working within corrections. This included how social workers navigated the dual axes of securitization—on the one hand, providing social work interventions in a securitized context and on the other hand, dealing with the inherent logic of prison systems and their punitive nature. Describing prisons as *total institutions*, the authors argued that such institutions can undermine social work principles such as voluntary commitment to engage in services or programming and, related to this, client-centered interventions and client consent (Jakob et al., 2023). Data from interviews with these social workers revealed that they faced difficulties establishing therapeutic alliances with clients while managing expectations from other stakeholders within the penal system. To address these challenges, social workers utilized key concepts such as trust-based relationships, transparency, reflexivity, and process orientation. Additionally, Jakob and colleagues found that reflexivity, emotion management, and being mindful of the security context and avoiding to adopt a logic of securitization were equally important for social workers practicing in this context. Proactively engaging with these tensions helped practitioners avoid fear and uncertainty that can undermine a constructive, authentic, and trusting working relationship with clients but also with stakeholders from other sectors. Providing training to correctional staff and trainees also helped build capacity including at the organizational level (Jakob et al., 2024). For example, professionals, including social workers, from CVE intervention programs were regularly involved in education for correctional personnel and therein advocated for an inclusive and equitable prison environment as a means to help prevent violent extremism (Jakob et al., 2024). Coaching for correctional professionals was also provided on a case-by-case basis to strengthen individual capacity and skill development (Jakob et al., 2024).

As discussed in Chap. 3, CVE case management-based interventions have received considerable attention over the last few years (Lewis et al., 2024). This extends into correctional contexts too, with case management being proposed as a best practice when working with convicted violent extremist offenders and individuals identified as at-risk of radicalization (Barracosa & March, 2022; Cherney, 2018; Cherney & Belton, 2021). Work undertaken in Australian contexts provides further insights into how case management-based interventions for CVE take shape within correctional contexts.

Barracosa and March, who examined lessons learned from the Australian juvenile justice CVE program in New South Wales, found that a multidisciplinary and non-punitive approach to supervision, client-focused assessment and case management was successful in addressing developmental and psychosocial vulnerabilities in addition to violent extremism risk factors among young offenders (Barracosa & March, 2022). The authors emphasized that careful planning and continuity of care are key organizational instruments—not only when transitioning offenders from youth to adult correctional systems, but also to sustain long-term disengagement and rehabilitation (Barracosa & March, 2022). This youth-focused justice CVE program, aimed at incarcerated youth at-risk of radicalization or who were sentenced for terrorism-related offences, includes comprehensive assessment and individually tailored case management plans: "These plans are designed to address developmental and psychosocial vulnerabilities, criminogenic risks, and protective or risk mitigating factors" (Barracosa & March, 2022, p. 5). Caseworkers and program facilitators support youth by addressing needs related to mental health, education, vocational training, leisure, community engagement, life-skills, and future planning, as well as extending services to the youths' families (Barracosa & March, 2022).

Much like the youth-focused model, the Proactive Integrated Support Model (PRISM) is implemented by Corrective Services New South Wales in Australia (Cherney, 2018). Launched as a pilot initiative in February 2016, PRISM is designed for incarcerated individuals either convicted of terrorism-related offenses or identified as being at risk of radicalization due to extremist beliefs or associations. Participation in PRISM is voluntary and facilitated by a multidisciplinary team that includes psychologists, a religious support officer, program and services staff, allied health professionals, and other relevant agencies. Together, they develop tailored case assessments and intervention plans.

Referrals to PRISM come from various sources, including the correctional intelligence group. Once an inmate consents to participate, a comprehensive risk and needs assessment is conducted to inform their individualized treatment goals. For example, findings from the program indicate that more than half of participants had experienced adversity during childhood, which was often linked to their radicalization pathways. Common traits among participants included histories of school misconduct, antisocial behavior, and violence (Cherney, 2018). Interventions are being customized to meet individual needs and this includes strategies to foster pro-social behaviors, including through religious mentoring, family involvement, educational and employment engagement, and increased awareness of peer influences.

A distinctive feature of PRISM is its integration of family members and community corrections personnel (e.g., parole and probation officers). This collaborative approach not only strengthened engagement with community corrections but also led to increased interest from staff in learning about the program and exploring partnership opportunities (Cherney, 2018). It is the role of social workers within PRISM in particular to work with family members of those incarcerated, conduct needs assessments, provide counseling, discharge planning, and service navigation.

Discharge from prison can take several forms, from temporary leaves, probation/parole, or full release at sentence expiry. Key to all of them is the goal of safe and successful reintegration into the community. As noted in other sections of this book, case management that is responsive to risk and need (Dyck et al., 2018) is a complex task that must be delivered diligently. Correctional workers may face intense pressure to ensure public safety, although they may find that there are less resources available to them due to the nature of their client's crime and associated stigma. Persons convicted of high-profile extremism related offenses, or the repatriation of extremist travelers (returnees) face particular challenges around public stigma. Police may issue public safety press releases when a prisoner achieves parole, or the return of an extremist traveler may only occur after intense political debate and media coverage. Clients and their families may be subjected to media interference in their personal lives, news coverage that digs up personal history and labels them a threat. Social services and CVE organizations can also be pursued by journalists for commentary. Social workers and CVE teams can mitigate these issues by maintaining confidentiality, advocating and even orienting relevant services (e.g., child welfare, schools), and providing guidance to clients on how to navigate stigma in the private market (e.g., challenges surrounding banking and housing).

4.5 Conclusion

This chapter emphasized the critical role of multi-sectoral and multi-agency collaboration in CVE efforts, particularly as these initiatives extend beyond national security and law enforcement domains. Multi-sectoral and multi-agency collaboration involves strengthening collaborative resource development across various groups, sectors, and disciplines through capacity building in high-need areas. However, such collaborations, described by Finn as environments for *teaching–learning*, might involve significant challenges stemming from power relations which might hinder critical dialogue and learning. Viewing such collaboration as a process and utilizing time and structured meetings to discuss ethics, roles, and responsibilities, lay the foundation for trust and inter-agency team-building. The importance of multi-sectoral collaboration was further underscored when working with children and youth, especially those at risk of radicalization or whose parents were involved in extremism. Adolescents can be particularly vulnerable to radicalization due to their developmental stage but also due to exposure to hateful and extremist content online. It was discussed how families can be supported through family dialogue and psychoeducation to discover not only risks but also needs and mobilize strengths and protective factors through collaborative action. Further, when parents or caregivers struggle with mental health challenges, providing clinical interventions can help them understand the impact of trauma, engage meaningfully in their child's healing process, and address their own emotional or cognitive responses. Lastly, this chapter discussed the challenges and opportunities of working in prisons and correctional contexts. Social workers in these settings are tasked with navigating the complexities of practicing in punitive and securitized environments, and supporting clients faced with social stigma. Despite these challenges, prisons and corrections contexts can also serve as places for positive change and multidisciplinary resourcing and programming. Holistic assessments, individually tailored case management, and trauma-informed care approaches were highlighted as beneficial strategies in these contexts. These approaches can help address the underlying trauma, adversities, and unmet needs of incarcerated individuals, facilitating their rehabilitation and reintegration into society and communities.

References

Argentino, M.-A., Barrett, G., & Tyler, M. B. (2024). *764: The intersection of terrorism, violent extremism, and child sexual exploitation*. Global Network on Extremism & Technology. Retrieved July 9, 2025, from https://gnet-research.org/2024/01/19/764-the-intersection-of-terrorism-violent-extremism-and-child-sexual-exploitation/

Barracosa, S., & March, J. (2022). Dealing with radicalised youth offenders: The development and implementation of a youth-specific framework. *Frontiers in Psychiatry, 12*, 773545. https://doi.org/10.3389/fpsyt.2021.773545

Berner, H. (2022). The prevention of extremism and the role of safety: Essay on a well-balanced relationship between social work and law enforcement. *European Journal for Security Research, 7*, 21–38. https://doi.org/10.1007/s41125-022-00082-y

Bjørgo, T. (2016). Counter-terrorism as crime prevention: A holistic approach. *Behavioral Sciences of Terrorism and Political Aggression, 8*(1), 25–44. https://doi.org/10.1080/19434472.2015.1108352

Campelo, N., Oppetit, A., Thompson, C., Cohen, D., & Louet, E. (2022). A clinical and psychopathological approach to radicalization among adolescents. *Frontiers in Psychiatry, 13*, 788154. https://doi.org/10.3389/fpsyt.2022.788154

Campion, K., & Colvin, E. (2024). Foreign and familiar: Recruitment pathways of young people engaged with extremism in Australia. *Perspectives on Terrorism, XVIII*(4), 1–20. https://doi.org/10.19165/2024.8828

Canadian Anti-Hate Network. (August 23, 2022). *Anti-Transgender Candidates Enter School Board Elections*. CAHN. Retrieved March 11, 2025, from https://www.antihate.ca/anti_transgender_candidates_enter_school_board_elections_ottawa.

Canadian Practitioners Network for the Prevention of Extremist Violence. (2024). *Executive summary. Report II. Collaborative models and challenges related to multisectoral collaboration in Canada*. CPN-PREV. Retrieved March 11, 2025, from https://static1.squarespace.com/static/668953bc9928de19ab00ca30/t/6689aa1c51c6376f58ca1ad8/1720298012936/Executive-summary-EN-04.21.2024.pdf.

Casey, B. J., Jones, R. M., & Hare, T. A. (2008). The adolescent brain. *Annals of the New York Academy of Sciences, 1124*, 111–126. https://doi.org/10.1196/annals.1440.010

Cherney, A., & Belton, E. (2021). The evaluation of case-managed programs targeting individuals at risk of radicalisation. *Terrorism and Political Violence, 35*(4), 846–865. https://doi.org/10.1080/09546553.2021.1984236

Cherney, A. (2018). Evaluating interventions to disengage extremist offenders: A study of the proactive integrated support model (PRISM). *Behavioral Sciences of Terrorism and Political Aggression, 12*(1), 17–36. https://doi.org/10.1080/19434472.2018.1495661

Chivers, C. (2018). 'What is the headspace they are in when they are making those referrals?' Exploring the lifeworlds and experiences of health and social care practitioners undertaking risk work within the prevent strategy. *Health, Risk & Society, 20*(1–2), 81–103. https://doi.org/10.1080/13698575.2018.1437121

Dyck, H. L., Campbell, M. A., & Wershler, J. L. (2018). Real-world use of the risk-need responsivity model and the level of service/case management inventory with community-supervised offenders. *Law and Human Behavior, 42*(3), 258–268. https://doi.org/10.1037/lhb0000279

Ellis, B. H., Miller, A. B., Schouten, R., Agalab, N. Y., & Abdi, S. M. (2022). The challenge and promise of a multidisciplinary team response to the problem of violent radicalization. *Terrorism and Political Violence, 34*(7), 1321–1338. https://doi.org/10.1080/09546553.2020.1777988

Erwin, D. (2016). *Young people and extremism: A resource pack for youth workers*. SALTO-Youth Cultural Diversity Resource Centre. Retrieved March 11, 2025, from https://www.salto-youth.net/downloads/4-17-3477/SALTO%20extremism%20pack.pdf.

Finn, J. L. (2021). *Just practice. A social justice approach to social work*. Oxford University Press.

Gavrielides, T. (2012). Contextualizing restorative justice for hate crime. *Journal of Interpersonal Violence, 27*(18), 3624–3643. https://doi.org/10.1177/0886260512447575

Gereluk, D. (2023). A whole-school approach to address youth radicalization. *Educational Theory, 73*(3), 434–451. https://doi.org/10.1111/edth.12581

Gheorghe, R. M. (2023). "Just Be White (JBW)": Incels, race and the violence of whiteness. *Affilia, 39*(1), 59–77. https://doi.org/10.1177/08861099221144275

Global Counterterrorism Forum. (2018). *The Hague good practices on the nexus between transnational organized crime and terrorism*. GCTF. Retrieved July 9, 2025, from https://www.thegctf.org/Portals/1/Documents/Framework%20Documents/2018/GCTF-Good-Practices-on-the-Nexus_ENG.pdf?ver=2018-09-21-122246-363.

Global Initiative Against Transnational Organized Crime. (2024). *Violent extremism and organized crime: Thematic series*. Global Initiative Against Transnational Organized Crime. Retrieved July 9, 2025, from https://globalinitiative.net/analysis/violent-extremism-and-organized-crime/.

Government of Canada (GOC). (2024). *Terrorism Peace bonds annual report—June 21, 2022 to June 20, 2023*. Retrieved July 9, 2025, from https://www.justice.gc.ca/eng/rp-pr/cj-jp/antiter/terrorism4-terrorisme4/index.html.

Hassan, G., Brouillette-Alarie, S., Ousman, S., Savard, É. L., Kilinc, D., Madriaza, P., Varela, W., Pickup, D., Danis, E., & The CPN-PREV Team. (2021). *A systematic review on the outcomes of tertiary prevention programs in the field of violent radicalization*. Canadian Practitioners Network for the Prevention of Radicalization and Extremist Violence. Retrieved March 11, 2025, from https://cpnprev.ca/systematic-review-3/.

Haugstvedt, H. (2022). The role of social support for social workers engaged in preventing radicalization and violent extremism. *Nordic Social Work Research, 12*(1), 166–179. https://doi.org/10.1080/2156857X.2020.1806102

Haugstvedt, H., & Tuastad, S. E. (2023). "It Gets a Bit Messy": Norwegian social workers' perspectives on collaboration with police and security service on cases of radicalisation and violent extremism. *Terrorism and Political Violence, 35*(3), 677–693. https://doi.org/10.1080/09546553.2021.197054

Haugstvedt, H., & Gunnarsdottir, H. M. (2023). Managing role expectations and emotions in encounters with extremism: Norwegian social workers' experiences. *Qualitative Social Work, 22*(1), 67–85. https://doi.org/10.1177/14733250211051410

Hutchinson, J., Yuzva Clement, D., Gheorghe, R. M., Kellum, L., & Shuttleworth, A. (2025). "I'm Not Super Familiar with Children's Ecosystems Online": Expert assessments on the effects of early childhood exposure to extremism online. *Perspectives on Terrorism, XIX*(1), 64–91. https://doi.org/10.19165/2025.5669

Jakob, M., Diegmann, D., Herdig, M., & Frank, A. (2024). *Innovation, Wirkungen, Transfer. Abschlussbericht der wissenschaftlichen Begleitung der Modellprojekte im Themenfeld "Prävention und Deradikalisierung in Strafvollzug und Bewährungshilfe" im Bundesprogramm "Demokratie leben!" in der Förderphase 2020 bis 2024*. Deutsches Jugendinstitut.

Jakob, M., Jukschat, N., & Leistner, A. (2023). The paradoxes of social work in a securitised setting: the example of prevention and radicalisation in German prisons. *International Journal of Social Pedagogy, 12*(1). https://doi.org/10.14324/111.444.ijsp.2023.v12.x.003

Koehler, D., Fiebig, V., & Jugl, I. (2023). From gaming to hating: Extreme-right ideological indoctrination and mobilization for violence of children on online gaming platforms. *Political Psychology, 44*, 419–434. https://doi.org/10.1111/pops.12855

Lewis, J., Marsden, S., Cherney, A., Zeuthen, M., Rahlf, L., Squires, C., & Peterscheck, A. (2024). Case management interventions seeking to counter radicalisation to violence and related forms of violence: A systematic review. *Campbell Systematic Reviews, 20*, e1386. https://doi.org/10.1002/cl2.1386

Livingstone, S., Kirwil, L., Ponte, C., & Staksrud, E. (2014). In their own words: What bothers children online? *European Journal of Communication, 29*(3), 271–288. https://doi.org/10.1177/0267323114521045

Lösel, F., King, S., Bender, D., & Jugl, I. (2018). Protective factors against extremism and violent radicalization: A systematic review of research. *International Journal of Developmental Science, 12*(1–2), 89–102. https://doi.org/10.3233/DEV-170241

McKenzie, A., & O'Brien, D. (2024). The evolution of estimated time of arrival: The city of Toronto's CVE program. *Journal for Deradicalization, 39*. https://journals.sfu.ca/jd/index.php/jd/article/view/911

RAN. (2018). *Vulnerable children who are brought up in an extremist environment. Ex post paper.* Radicalisation Awareness Network. Retrieved March 11, 2025, from https://home-affairs.ec.europa.eu/system/files_en?file=2018-09/ran_yf-c_vulnerable_children_who_brought_up_extremist_environment_21-22_06_2018_en.pdf.

RAN. (2019). *Children growing up in extremist families. Ex post paper*. Radicalisation Awareness Network. Retrieved March 11, 2025, from https://home-affairs.ec.europa.eu/system/files/2019-07/ran_yfc_children_growing_upin_extremist_families_24-25_04_2019_en.pdf

RAN. (2021). *Returning FTFs and their families: Practitioners' insights in improving the return process*. Radicalisation Awareness Network. Retrieved March 11, 2025, from https://home-affairs.ec.europa.eu/system/files/2021-12/ran_rehabilitation_returning_ftfs_and_their_families_16092021_en.pdf.

RCMP. (2024). *Five-eyes insights—young people and violent extremism: A call for collective action.* Royal Canadian Mounted Police. Retrieved March 11, 2025, from https://rcmp.ca/en/corporate-information/publications-and-manuals/five-eyes-insights-young-people-and-violent-extremism-call-collective-action.

Regehr, C., Kanani, K., McFadden, J., & Saini, M. (2016). *Essential law for social work practice in Canada* (3rd ed.). Oxford University Press.

Rousseau, C., Miconi, D., Johnson-Lafleur, J., Desmarais, C., & Hassan, G. (2024). Children of extremist parents: Insights from a specialized clinical team. *Clinical Child Psychology and Psychiatry, 29*(2), 687–699. https://doi.org/10.1177/13591045231192340

Rousseau, C., Miconi, D., Frounfelker, R. L., Hassan, G., & Oulhote, Y. (2020). A repeated cross-sectional study of sympathy for violent radicalization in Canadian college students. *American Journal of Orthopsychiatry, 90*(4), 406–418. https://doi.org/10.1037/ort0000444

Sapolsky, R. M. (2017). *Behave: The biology of humans at our best and worst.* Penguin Pr.

Schermaier-Stoeckl, B., Nadar, M., & Yuzva Clement, D. (2018). "Die nächste Generation?" - religiös-rigoristische Erziehung im salafistischen Kontext als Herausforderung für die erzieherische Kinder- und Jugendhilfe. *FORUM Jugendhilfe, 3*, 44–53.

Schlegel. L., Moonshot, W. J., & Regeni, P. (2025). *Implementing positive gaming interventions: A toolkit for practitioners.* RUSI. Retrieved March 11, 2025, from https://static.rusi.org/implementing-positive-gaming-interventions-toolkit_0.pdf.

Schlegel, L., & Kowert, R. (2024). *Gaming and Extremism. The Radicalization of Digital PlayGrounds*. Routledge.

Sivenbring, J., & Malmros, R. A. (2019). *Mixing logics. Multiagency approaches for countering violent extremism.* Segerstedt Institutet.

Smith, P. (2025). *Com/764: Transnational abuse, extortion, and cybercrime networks targeting youth.* Canadian Anti-Hate Network. Retrieved August 22, 2025, from https://assets.nationbuilder.com/antihate/pages/3562/attachments/original/1754415407/Com_764_-_Transnational_Abuse__Extortion__and_Cybercrime_Networks_Targeting_Youth.pdf?1754415407.

Stanley, T., Guru, S., & Coppock, V. (2017). A risky time for Muslim families: Professionalised counter-radicalisation networks. *Journal of Social Work Practice, 31*(4), 477–490. https://doi.org/10.1080/02650533.2017.1394829

Stanley, T., Guru, S., & Gupta, A. (2018). Working with PREVENT: Social work options for cases of 'Radicalisation Risk'. *Practice, 30*(2), 131–146. https://doi.org/10.1080/09503153.2017.1414176

Stanley, T., & Barracosa, S. (2024). Responding to radicalisation and extremism risk for youth: An emerging child protection and youth justice practice issue in Aotearoa. *Aotearoa New Zealand Social Work, 36*(3), 83–88. https://doi.org/10.11157/anzswj-vol36iss3id1161

United Nations Office on Drugs and Crime. (2016). *Handbook on the Management of Violent Extremist Prisoners and the Prevention of Radicalization to Violence in Prisons*. United Nations Office on Drugs and Crime.

van de Weert, A., & Eijkman, Q. A. M. (2019). Subjectivity in detection of radicalisation and violent extremism: A youth worker's perspective. *Behavioral Sciences of Terrorism and Political Aggression, 11*(3), 191–214. https://doi.org/10.1080/19434472.2018.1457069

van de Weert, A., & Eijkman, Q. A. M. (2021). Reconsidering early detection in countering radicalization by local frontline professionals. *Terrorism and Political Violence, 33*(2), 397–408. https://doi.org/10.1080/09546553.2021.1880237

van de Weert, A. (2022). Justice and risk assessment: the subjectivity of pre-emptive screening of radicalisation processes. *Journal of Policing, Intelligence and Counter Terrorism, 17*(3), 287–300. https://doi.org/10.1080/18335330.2022.2124123

Walkenhorst, D., Baaken, T., Ruf, M., Leaman, M., Handle, J., & Korn, J. (2020). *RAN rehabilitation manual—rehabilitation of radicalised and terrorist offenders for the first line practitioners*. Radicalisation Awareness Network. Retrieved March 11, 2025, from https://home-affairs.ec.europa.eu/networks/radicalisation-awareness-network-ran/publications/rehabilitation-manual-rehabilitation-radicalised-and-terrorist-offenders-first-line-practitioners_en.

Yuzva Clement, D. (2022). Post-migrant dynamics of Islam: Muslim youth and Salafism in Germany. In S. Zarrabi-Zadeh, T. K. Gugler, & A. Omerika (Eds.), *Dynamics of Islam in the modern world* (pp. 141–174). Brill. https://doi.org/10.1163/9789004512535_008

Yuzva Clement, D., Kiefer, J., Hassan, G., & King, M. (2022). Countering radicalization to violence in Canada. A multi-sector perspective. In R. Ceylan & M. Kiefer (Eds.), *Der islamische Fundamentalismus im 21. Jahrhundert. Analyse extremistischer Gruppen in westlichen Gesellschaften* (pp. 325–345). Springer VS. https://doi.org/10.1007/978-3-658-37486-0_16

Chapter 5
Outlook

In an era where the fabric of society is increasingly frayed by polarization, hate, and violent extremism—underpinned by increased loneliness, us-versus-them thinking, technological advancements in the digital realm, and global crises—the role and emerging leadership of social work in countering these forces emerges not only as a professional duty but as a profound ethical commitment. It was the objective of this book to illuminate the transformative potential of social work in providing holistic interventions, social reintegration, and psychosocial support to individuals at-risk of radicalization as well as individuals already engaged and entrenched in violent extremism, all the while keeping family-based approaches and multi-sectoral contexts in mind. Rooted in critical multisystemic approaches and social justice values, social work brings expertise in addressing individuals' risks, needs, and strengths through tailored, evidence-based approaches. As this book has highlighted, this work is most effective when carried out in collaboration with other professionals across sectors.

In today's world, it seems especially important to strengthen family bonds and support caregivers not just when their children and teenagers are exposed to extremist narratives, disinformation, and harmful influencers online, but also as pre-teens who are spending increased and significant time in digital spaces—often without adult supervision and guidance. Providing an advanced understanding regarding the intricacies of our digital worlds seems paramount, which means that social workers themselves have to upskill in this area, too. We should also not neglect the fact that adults engage and create meaning within digital ecosystems just like their younger counterparts. As social workers, understanding the allure and dynamics of digital communication and online communities is crucial when working with youth, parents and caregivers, and community stakeholders. This includes recognizing the pull factors such as social belonging, status-seeking, peer group validation, and thrill-seeking that influence digitized and algorithmically influenced youth behavior. Moreover, given that loneliness and social isolation can significantly impact physical and mental health, leading to anxiety, depression, and even suicidal

D. Yuzva Clement et al., *Social Work and Countering Violent Extremism*, SpringerBriefs in Social Work, https://doi.org/10.1007/978-3-032-07086-9_5

thoughts, addressing these issues is essential because they are often a core element of digital engagement but also radicalization. Studies have shown that youth today are evermore lonelier compared to previous decades despite or because of being "connected" in the cyberspace. As such, addressing radicalization also includes mitigating the over-reliance on digital devices, providing comprehensive digital literacy and critical thinking skills, as well as increasing interpersonal social relations and community activities where self-esteem, belonging, and positive recognition of own strengths and skills can develop and flourish. Formalizing *online ecology competence* could therefore become a core professional standard. Minimum proficiency should include platform ethnography, risk-signal recognition (e.g., extremist meme taxonomies, gaming chat cues), understanding digital capitalism, and advocacy capacity to influence *safety by design* conversations with tech stakeholders.

Against this complex backdrop, the concepts of radicalization, violent extremism, and associated terminologies are not static; they are dynamic and contested, evolving within the socio-political and socio-digital currents of our times. There is opportunity for social work researchers to contribute toward theory development and the refining of terminology that more accurately reflects the human experience of why and how people are drawn and involved in extremism and associated violence.

For the CVE field in general, proactively integrating social workers and drawing on social work scholarship can substantially enhance the effectiveness and ethical grounding of prevention and intervention efforts, while also contributing to the professionalization and institutional maturity of the field; the lessons from this book highlight that there are now a series of evidence-based models rooted in social work principles that should be top of mind for CVE practitioners, researchers, and policymakers. Social workers possess a wealth of clinical tools for designing and providing complex psychosocial interventions that are invaluable in addressing the multifaceted and dynamic challenges posed by violent extremism. The field of online violence prevention and reaching at-risk users online has also widened in recent years, showing promising effects. However, to effectively counter radicalization, it is imperative that social workers deepen their understanding of radicalization as a socio-emotional process, not merely a political one. This involves recognizing how radicalization evolves through emotional and psychological pathways, most often intertwined with personal and social grievances. Additionally, social workers should stay informed about both historical and emerging extremist movements and trends, particularly that drive individuals toward them. By expanding their knowledge in these areas, social workers can develop more nuanced and effective interventions that address the root causes of radicalization and promote sustainable social reintegration and disengagement from extremist ideologies and their social avenues.

To achieve this, social work faculties ought to enhance their curricula to include comprehensive training on preventing and countering violent extremism (P/CVE). For instance, curricular innovation could move beyond single elective units toward a more scaffolded learning design: a second-year foundational module on violence, inequality, and digital risk; followed by a third-year skills lab using mixed-reality simulations of extremist recruitment chats and online grooming; and a final-year capstone integrated field placement in a P/CVE or restorative-justice agency, accompanied by structured reflective journaling and supervision. Corresponding research programs could include the longitudinal evaluation of multisystemic CVE case management models, critical inquiry into the unintended consequences of securitised social policy, studying social workers' upskilling in digital competence and reaching at-risk users in online communities, or examining the clinical encounters unfolding between social workers and extremist clients. Furthermore, practicing social workers similarly need specialized education on radicalization processes and effective multi-sectoral collaboration. In this work, tensions are expected to arise, particularly when social workers collaborate with law enforcement or security institutions including in correctional or criminal justice contexts. Despite these potential tensions, adherence to legal statutes, professional standards of practice, and social work values and ethics can provide grounding frameworks for effective partnerships and multi-sectoral collaboration. As historical leaders in system navigation, complex practice environments, and client autonomy, social workers should lean into these tensions to ensure client rights are protected. Given the rise of a polarized culture, it is prudent to add curricula that feature how to navigate one's own triggers and practice boundaries and well-being when working in this realm. As discussed in this book, research has indeed found that practicing with clients espousing violent extremism can be challenging for frontline practitioners; using peer coaching, establishing a community of practice, and engaging in clinical supervision can help mitigate these triggers in social workers.

Finally, CVE is a diverse and multifaceted field, with varying approaches and networks across different countries. Violent extremism is a global phenomenon, which underscores the need for international collaboration and knowledge exchange for developing effective prevention and intervention strategies. In some jurisdictions, specialized nongovernmental organizations (NGOs) are dedicated to CVE efforts, while in others, community-based social service providers play a central role. Additionally, certain countries have established CVE programs within their corrections systems, whereas others have not. This diversity necessitates that social workers acquire localized knowledge of the specific networks and approaches within their countries or cities. Understanding the unique landscape of CVE initiatives, including the roles of NGOs, community services, law enforcement, and corrections programs, is essential for social workers to effectively engage in and contribute to these efforts. By becoming familiar with local and national CVE strategies, being mindful of urban versus rural or remote contexts, and building collaborative relationships across sectors, social workers can enhance their impact and emerging leadership in preventing and countering violent extremism within their communities.

Index

D. Yuzva Clement et al., *Social Work and Countering Violent Extremism*, SpringerBriefs in Social Work, https://doi.org/10.1007/978-3-032-07086-9

MIX
Papier aus verantwortungsvollen Quellen
Paper from responsible sources
FSC® C105338

If you have any concerns about our products,
you can contact us on
ProductSafety@springernature.com

In case Publisher is established outside the EU,
the EU authorized representative is:
Springer Nature Customer Service Center GmbH
Europaplatz 3, 69115 Heidelberg, Germany

Printed by Libri Plureos GmbH
in Hamburg, Germany